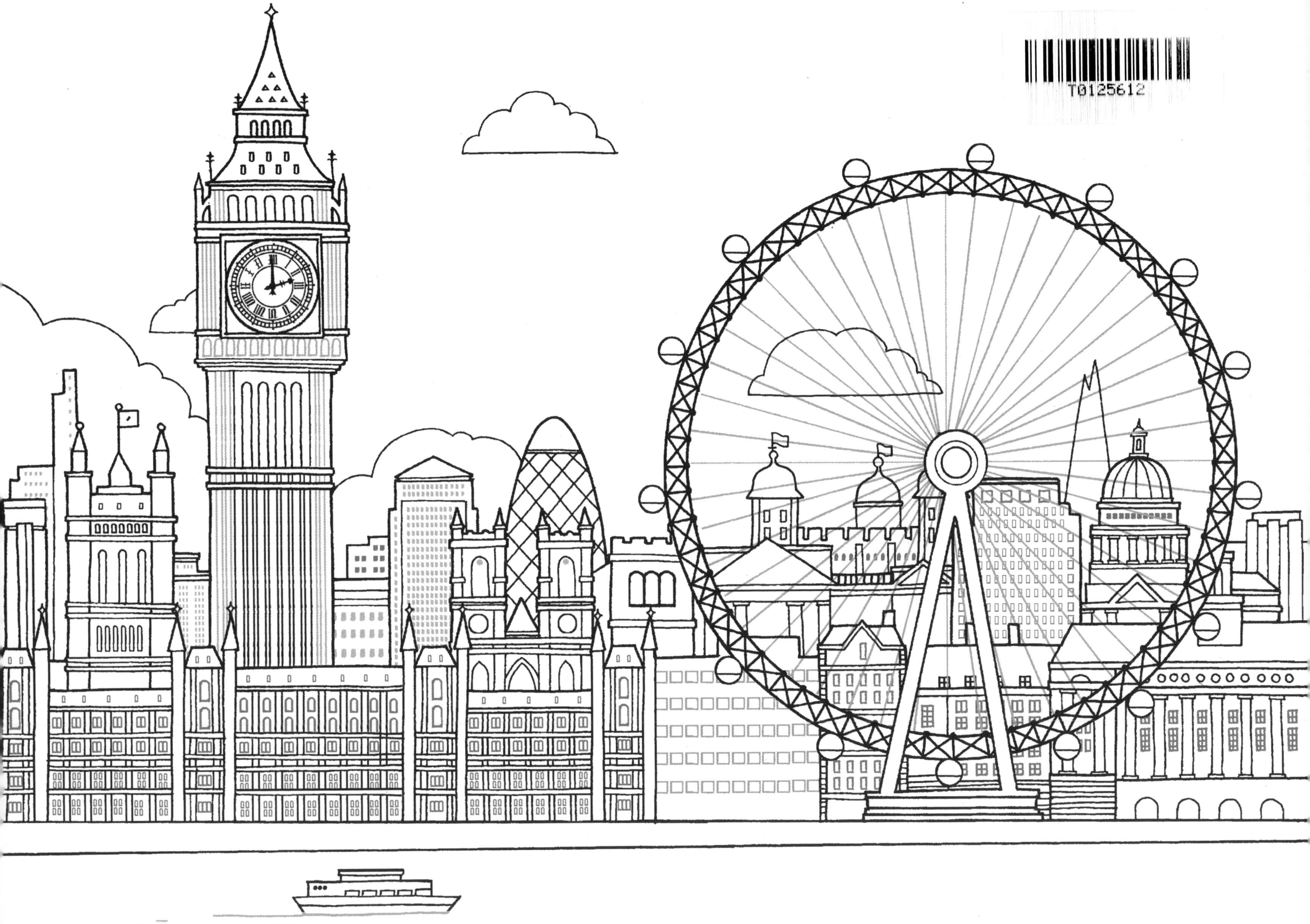

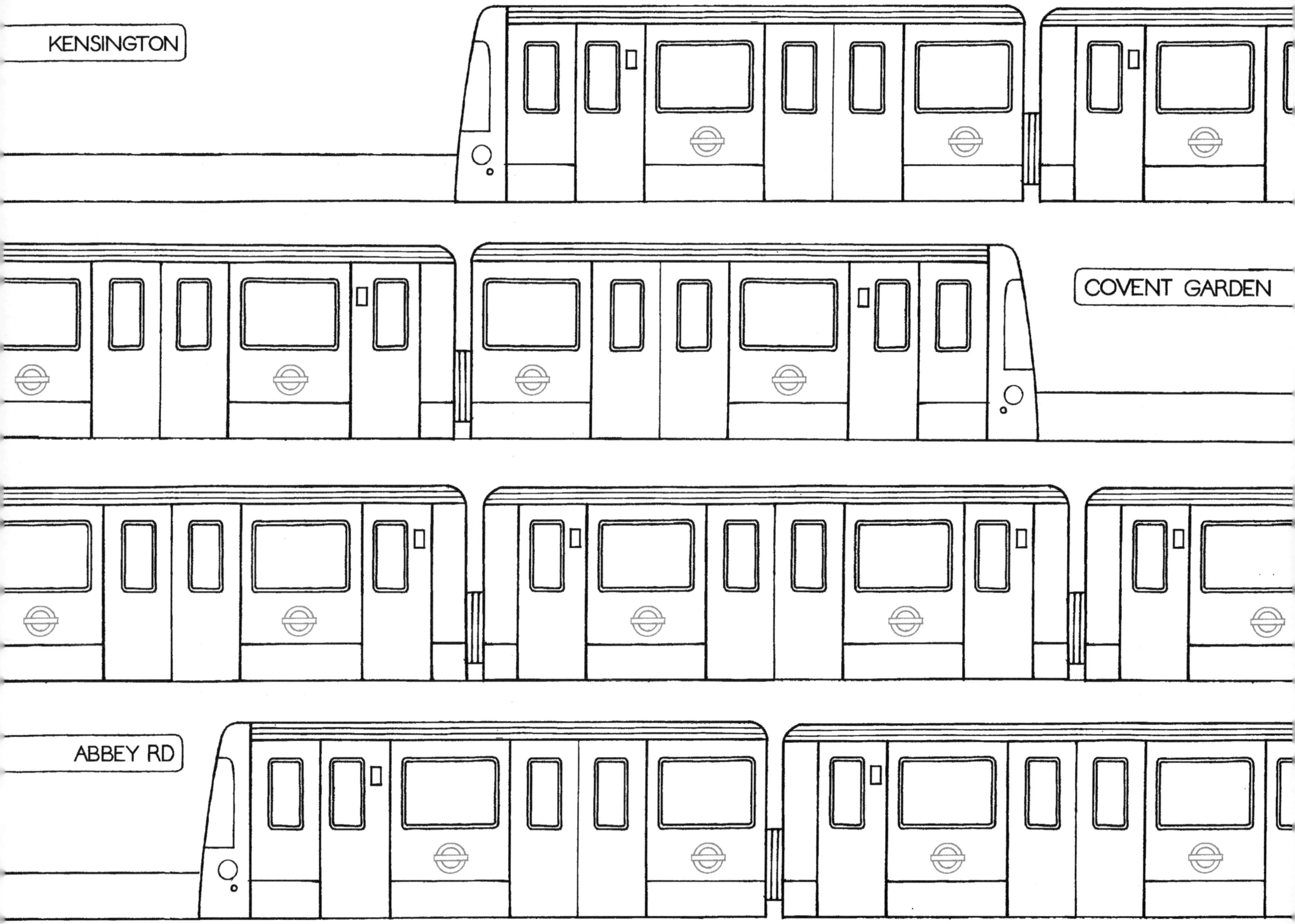
KENSINGTON
COVENT GARDEN
ABBEY RD

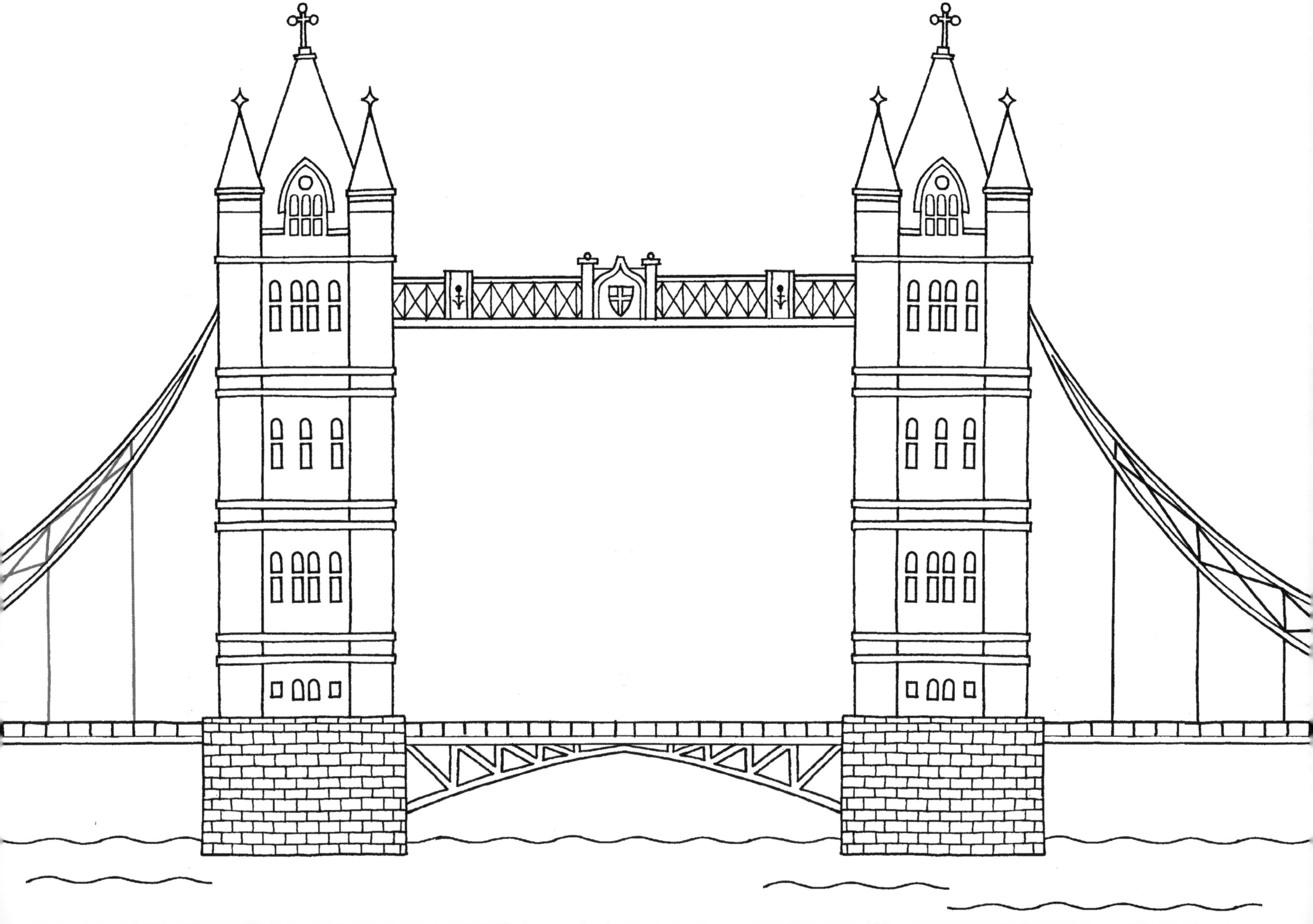

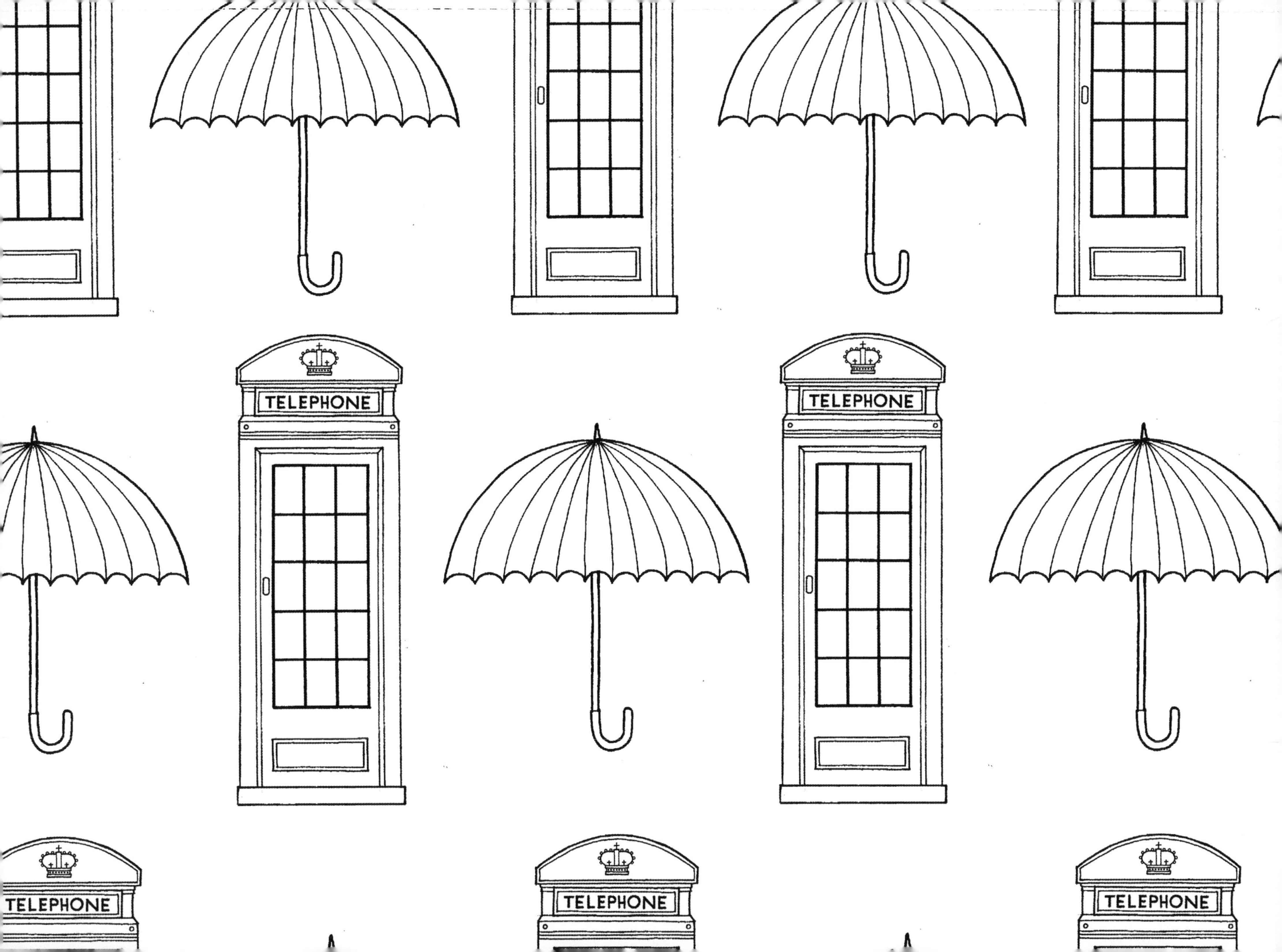
TELEPHONE
TELEPHONE
TELEPHONE
TELEPHONE
TELEPHONE

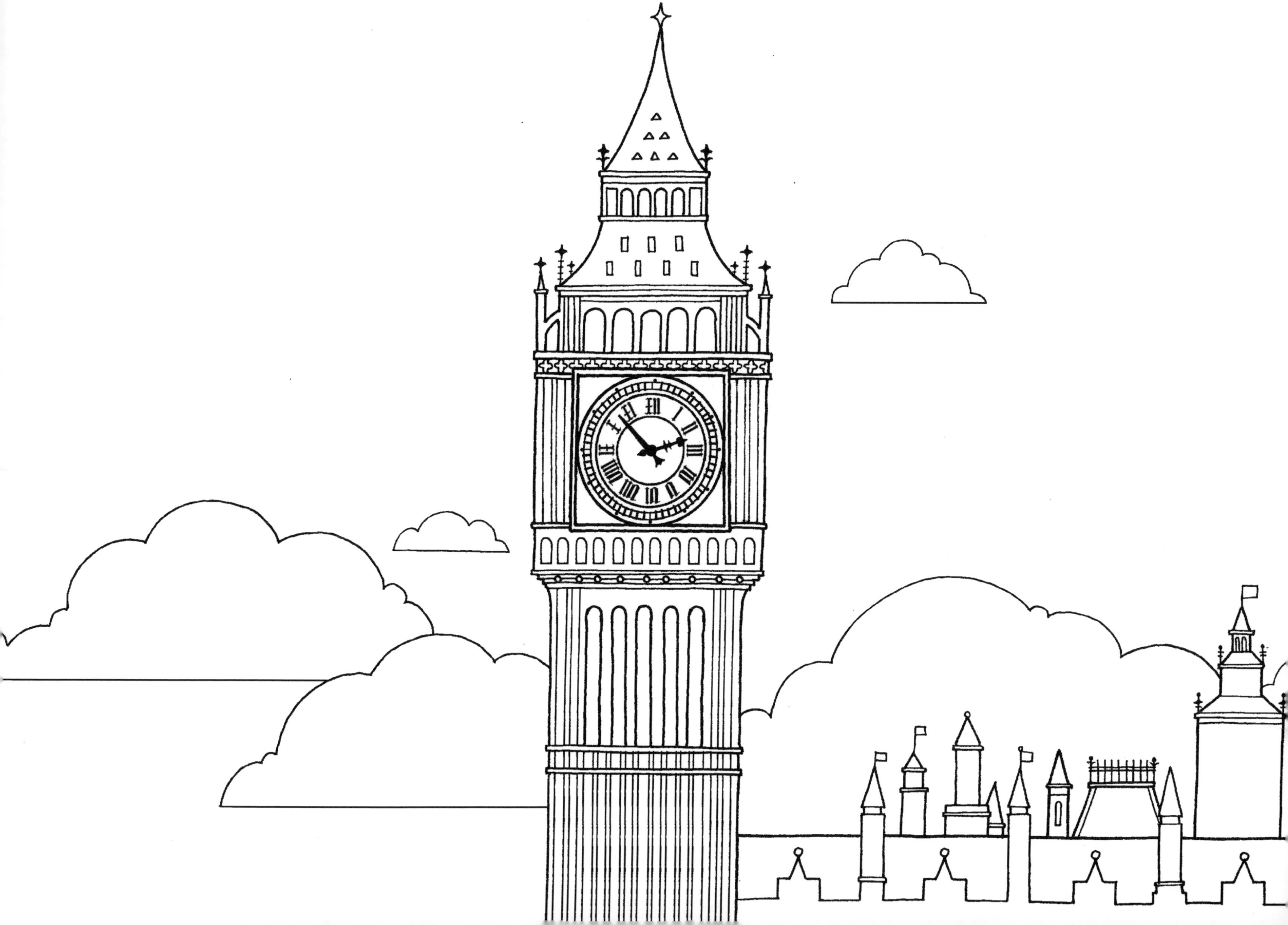

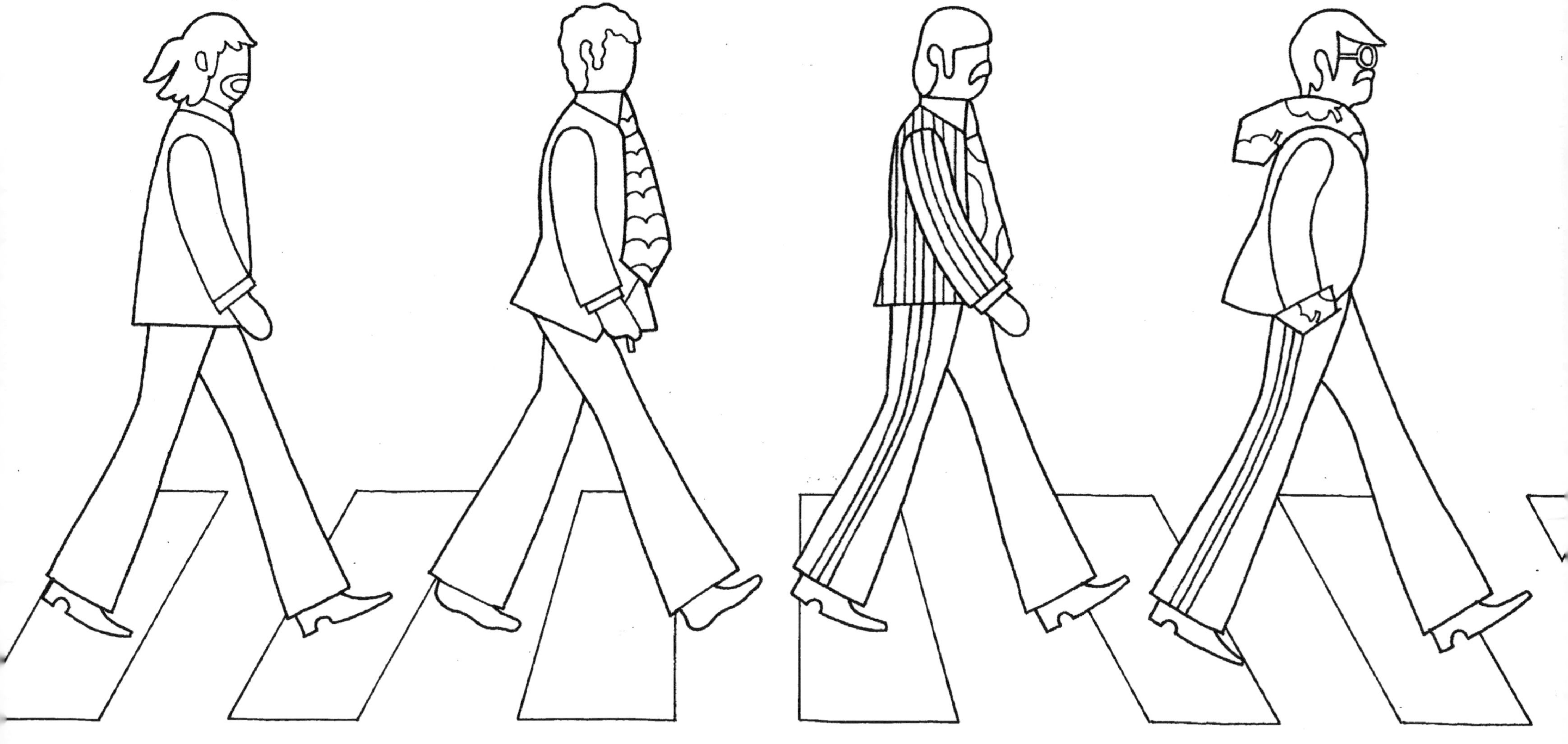

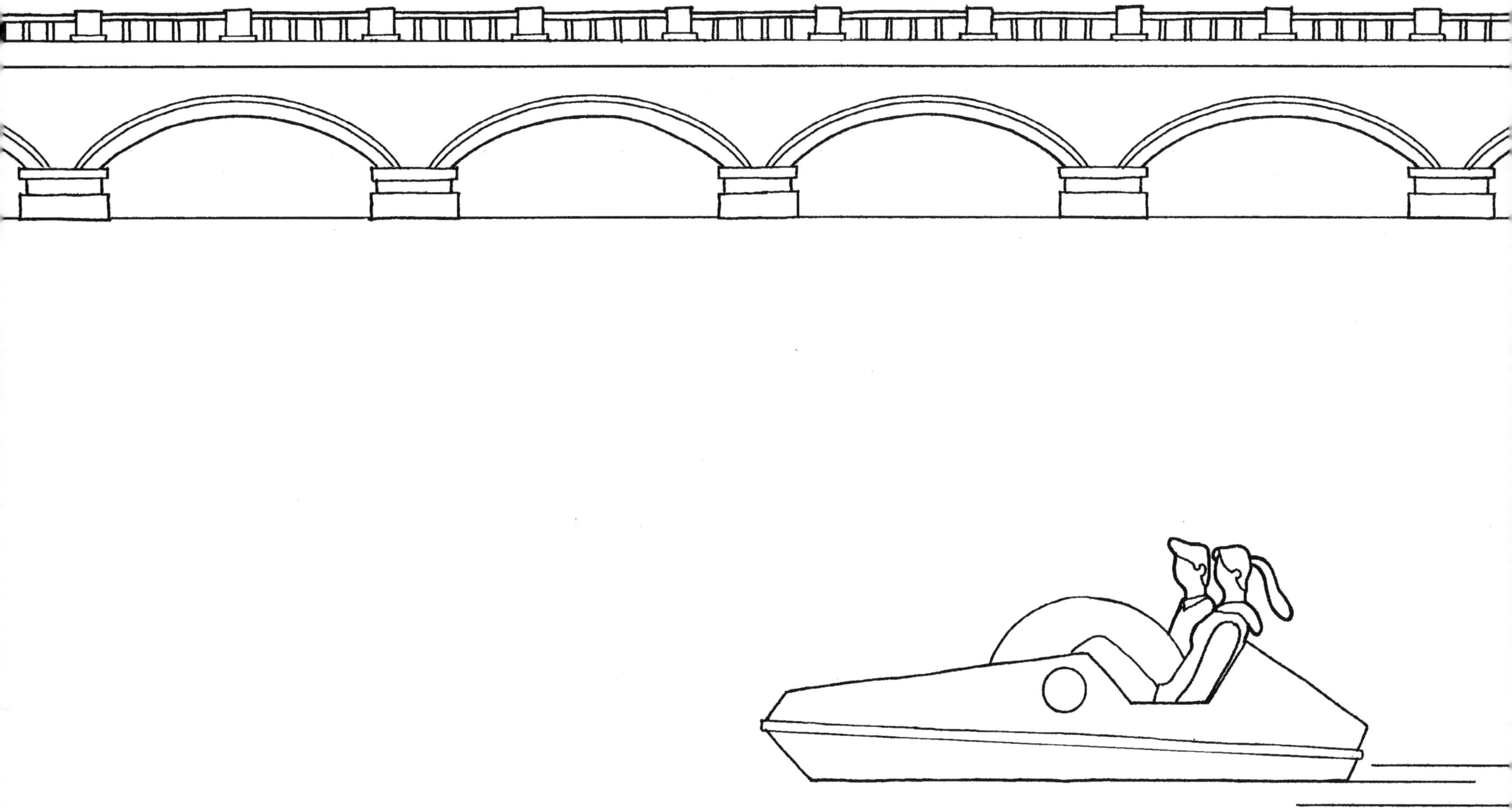

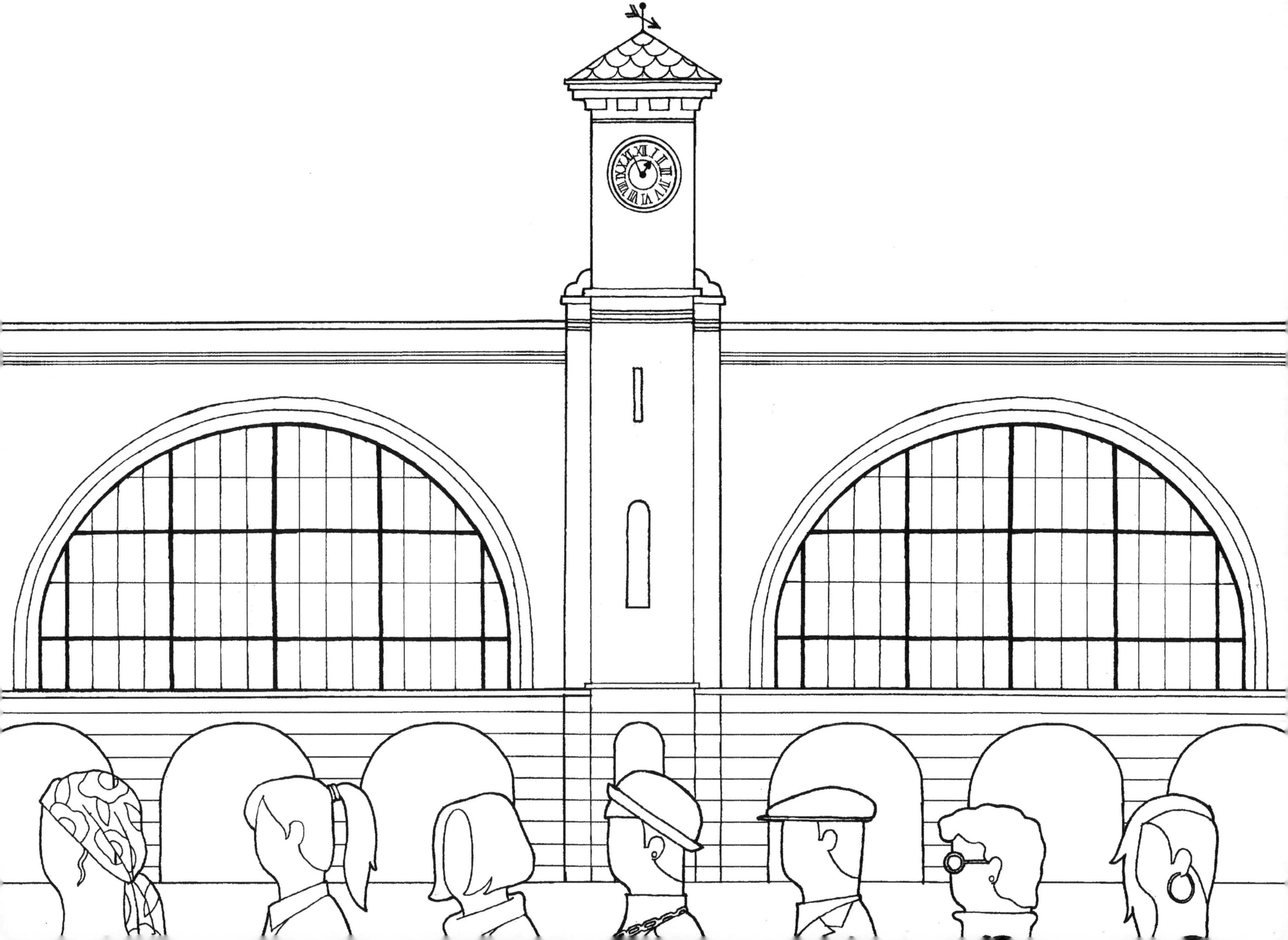

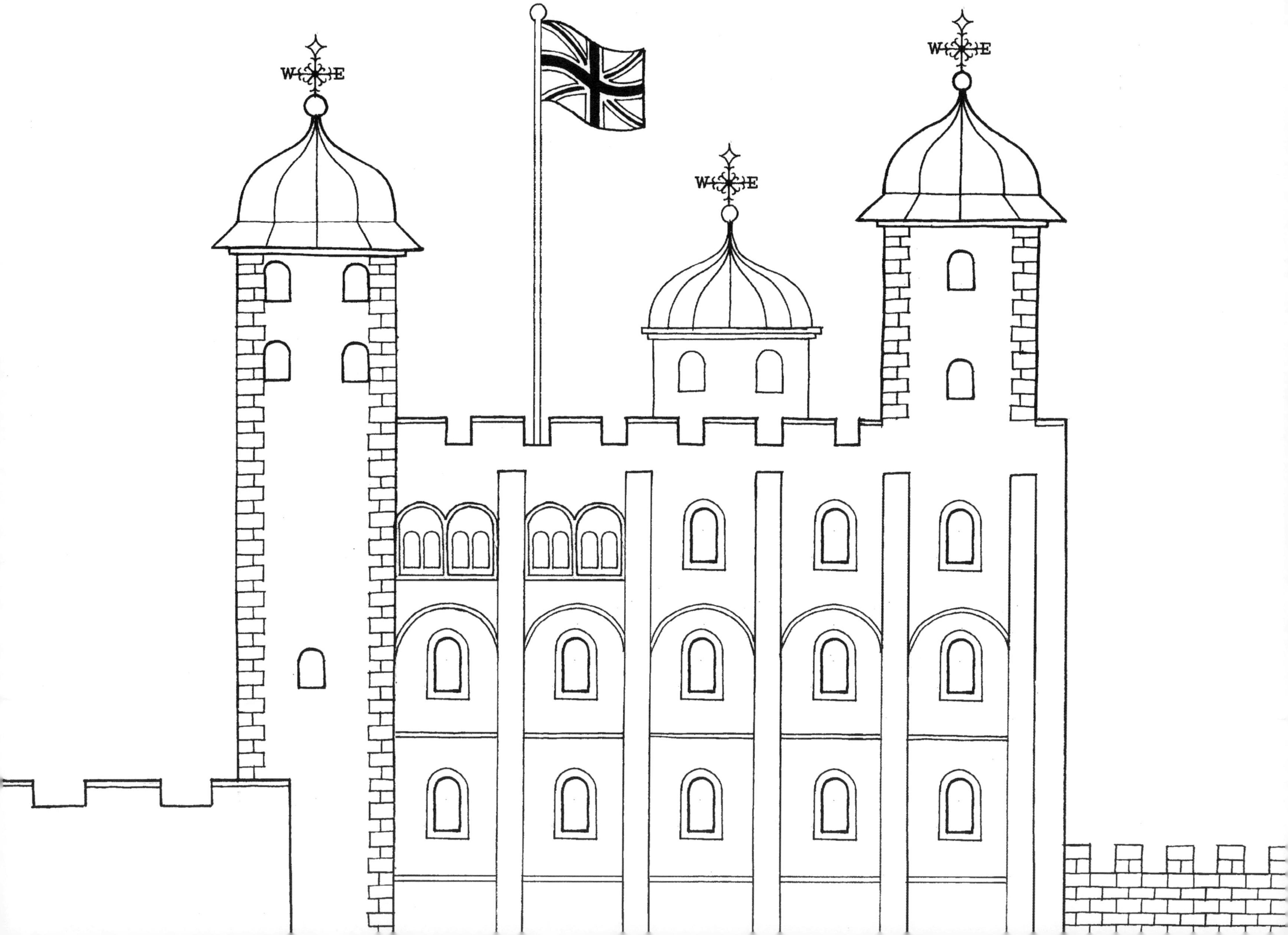
W E
W E
W E

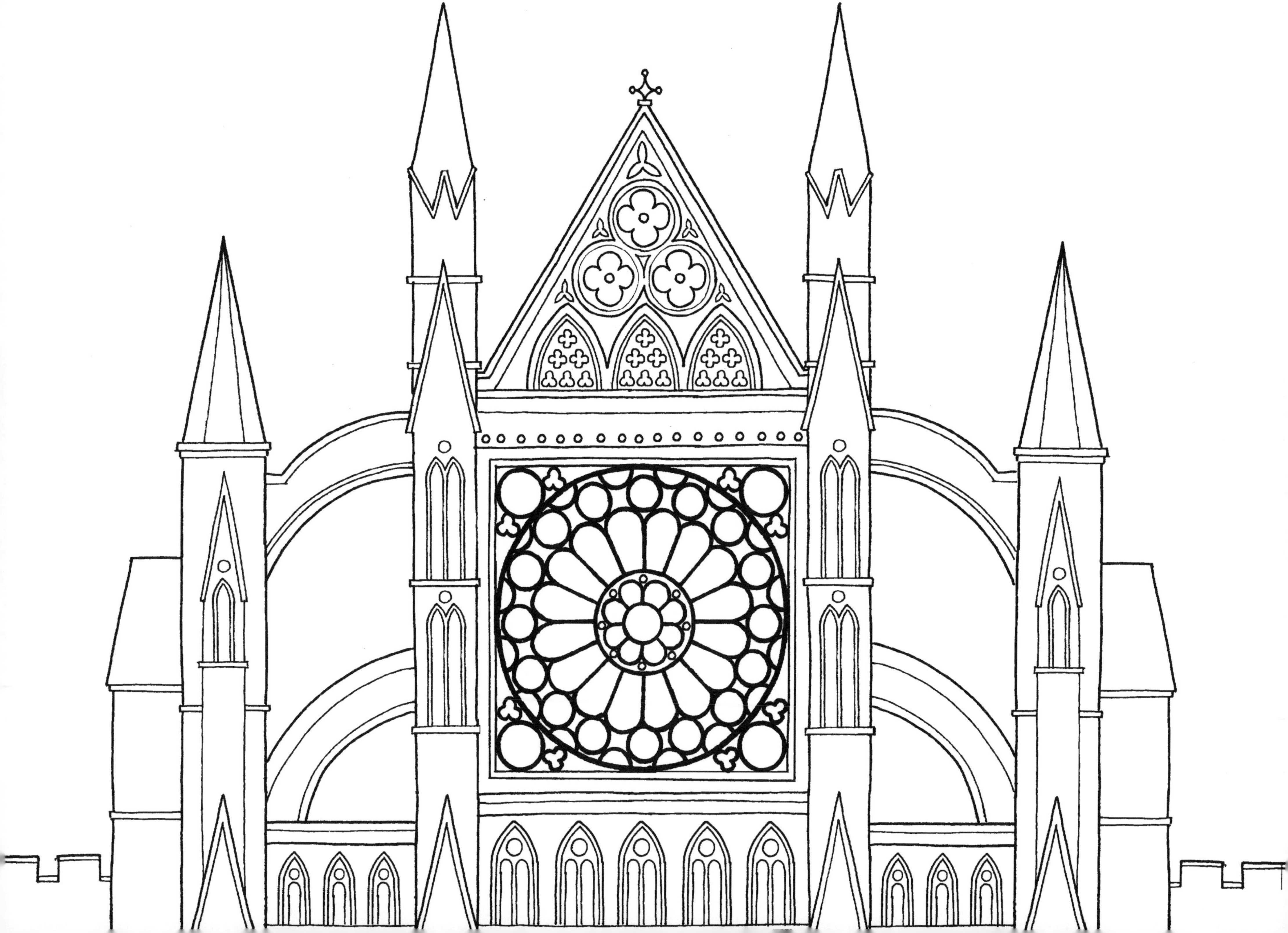

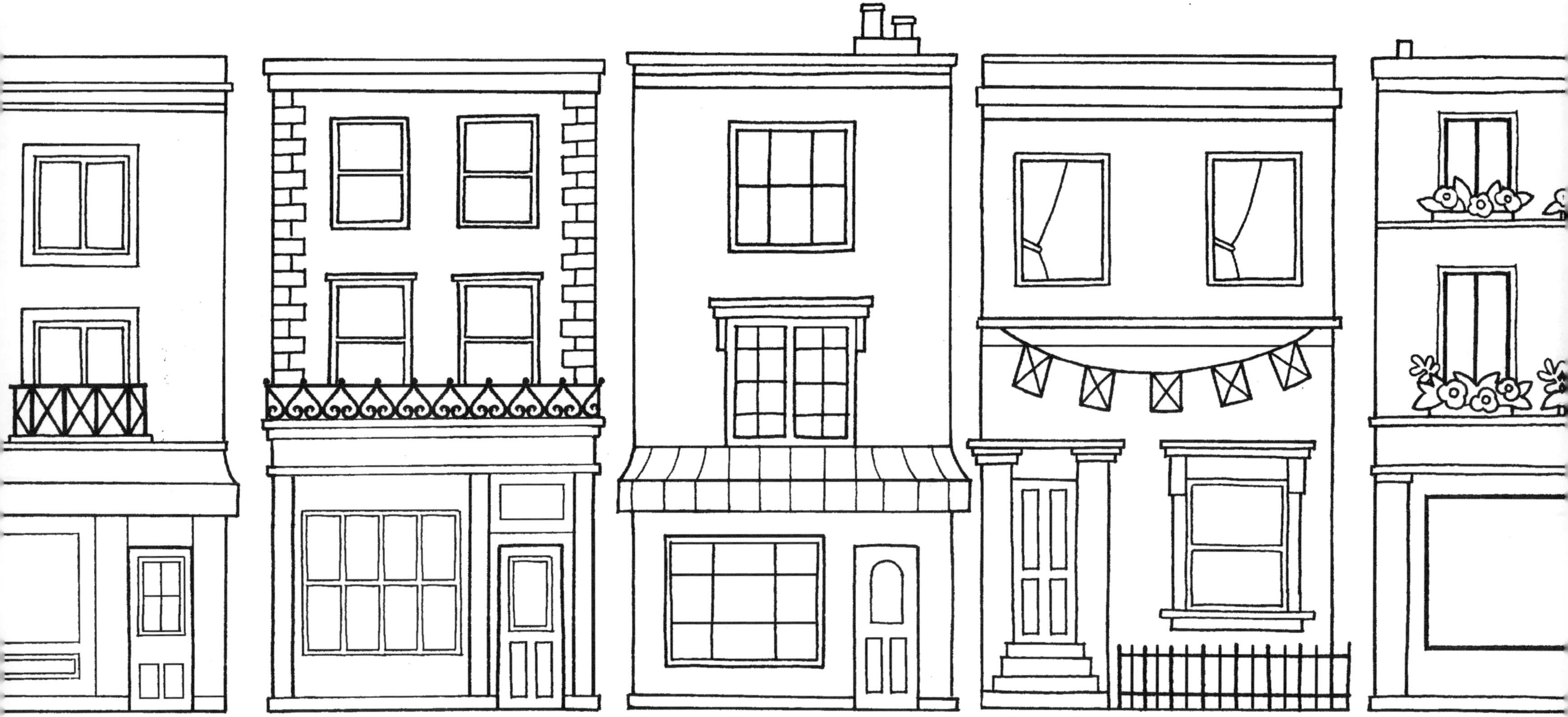

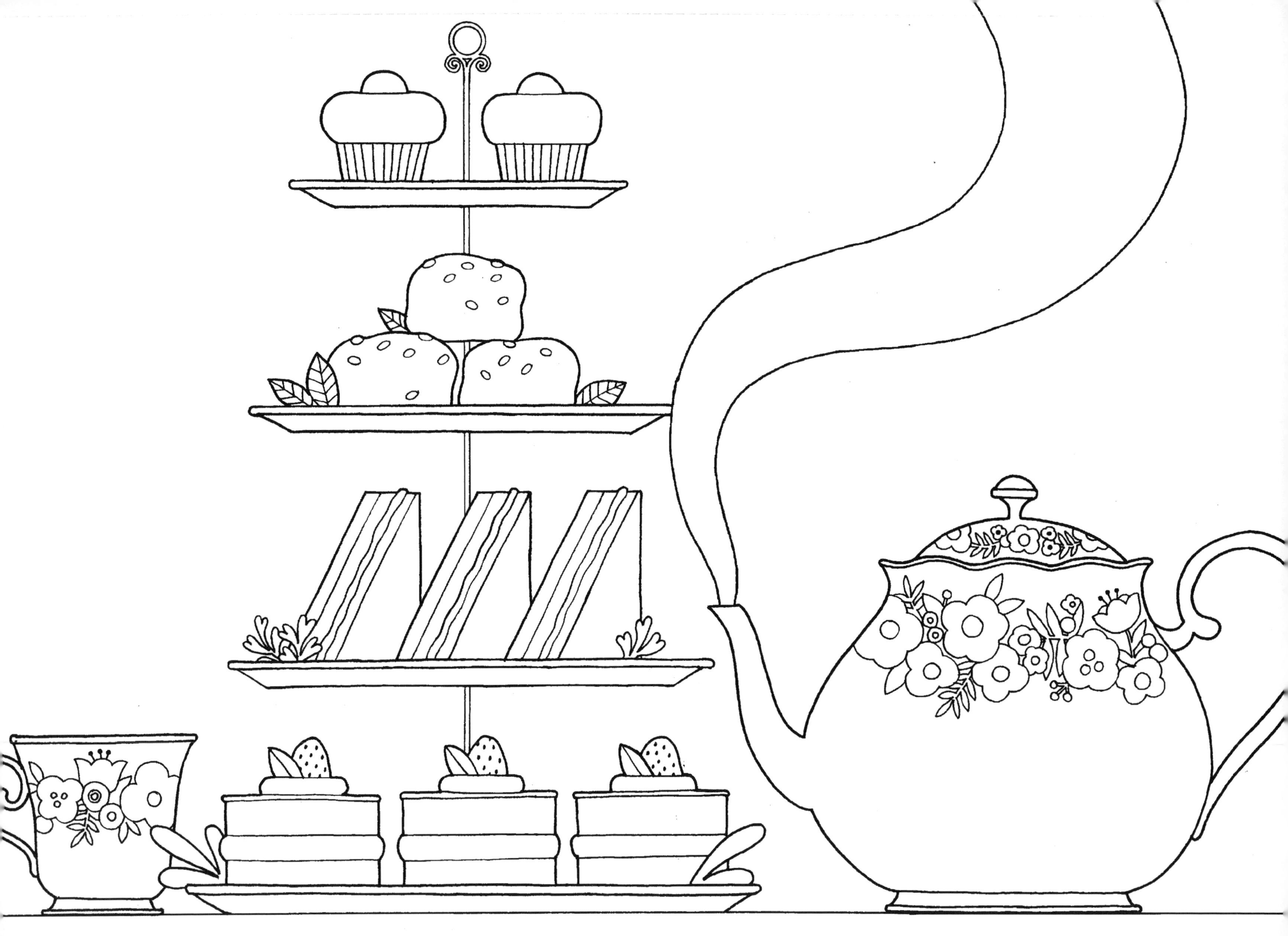

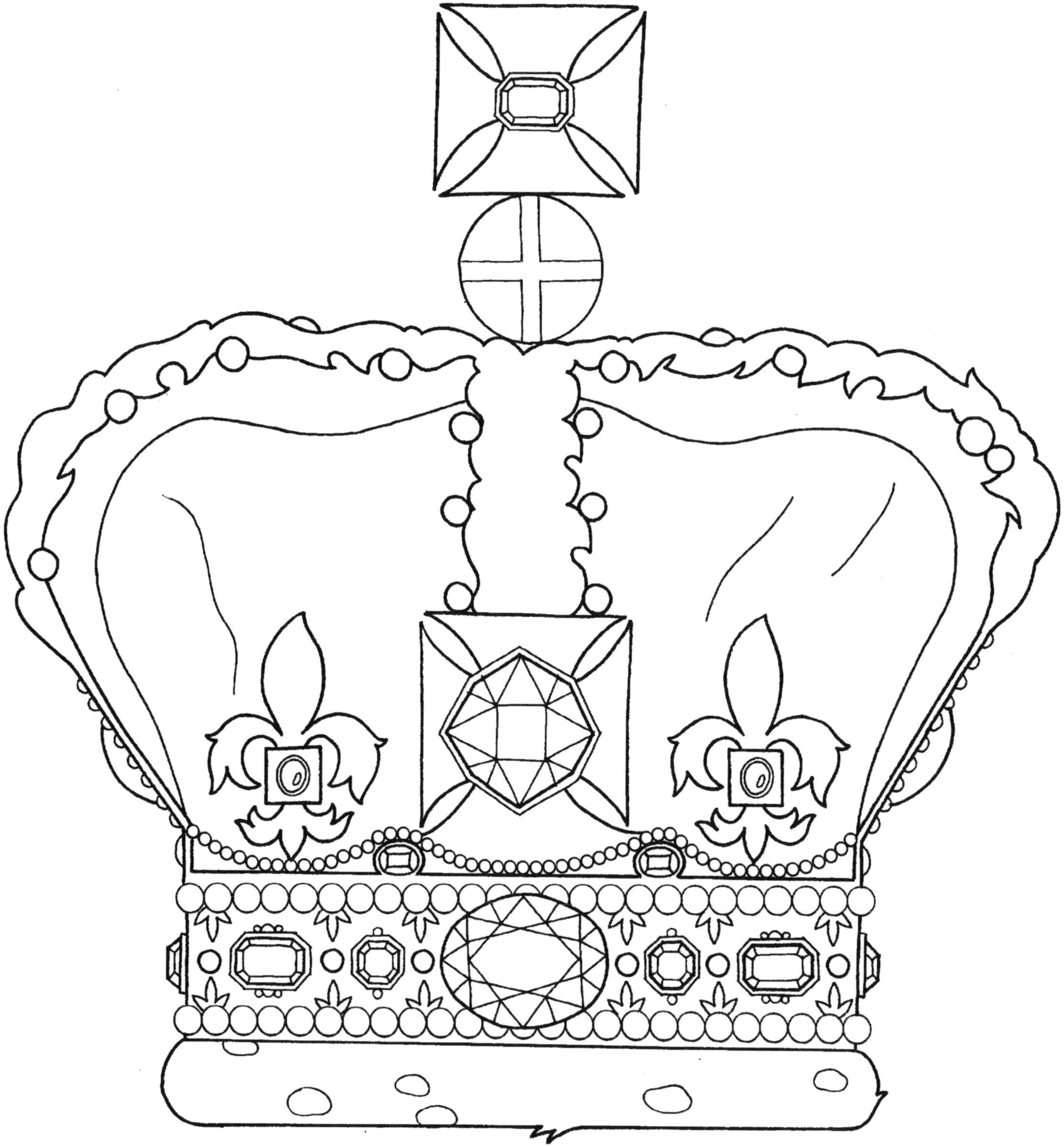

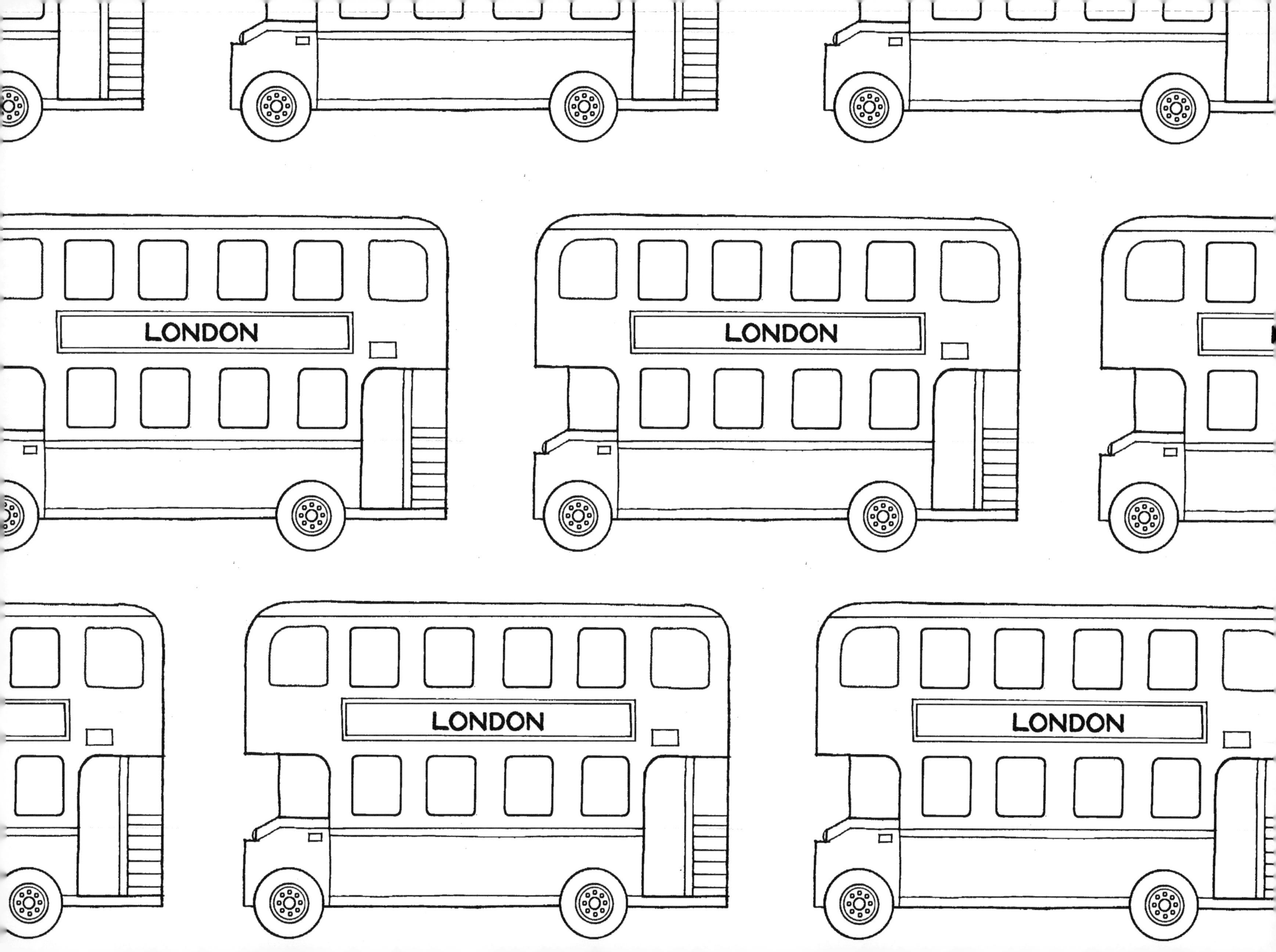
LONDON
LONDON
LONDON
LONDON

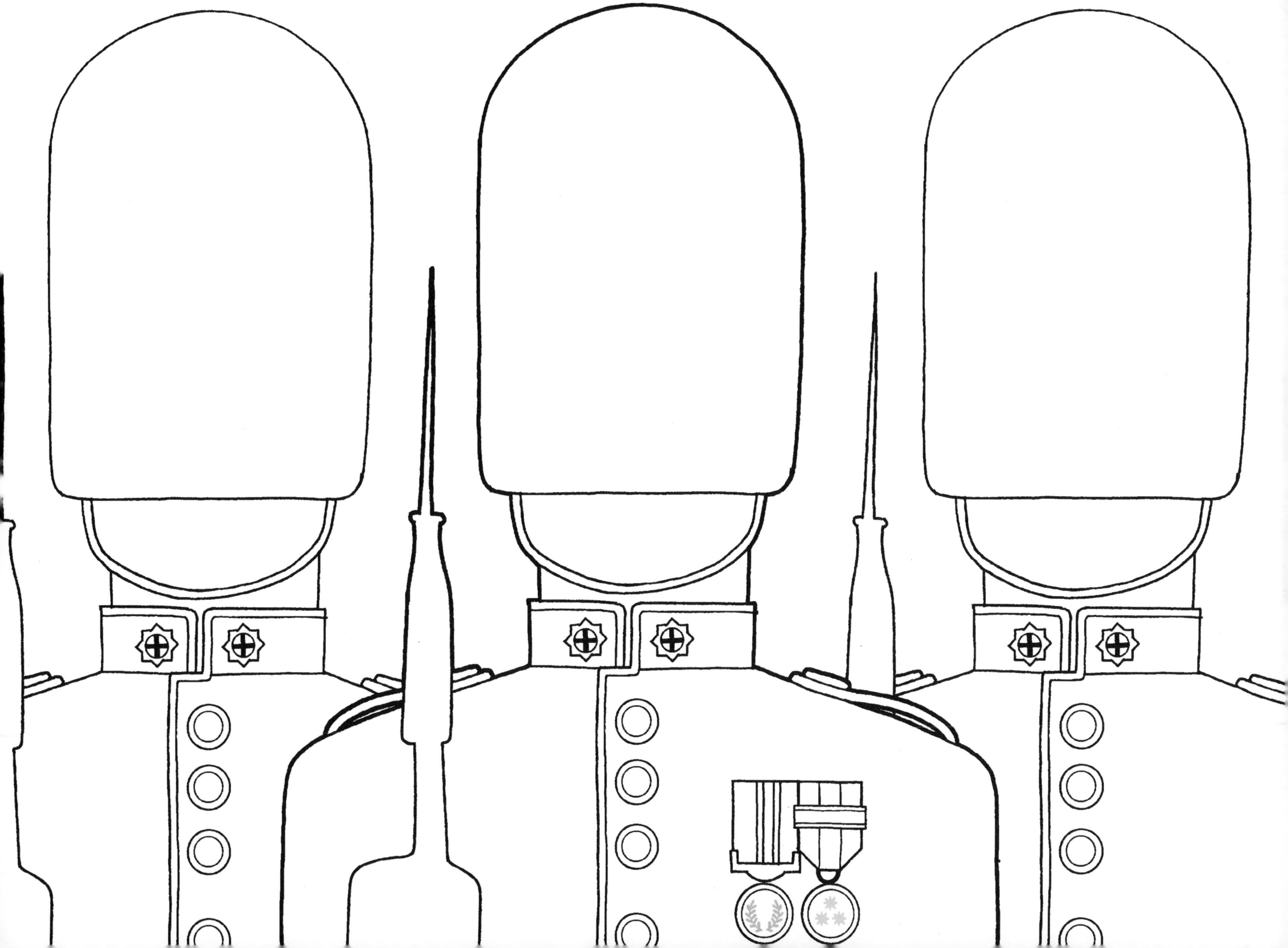

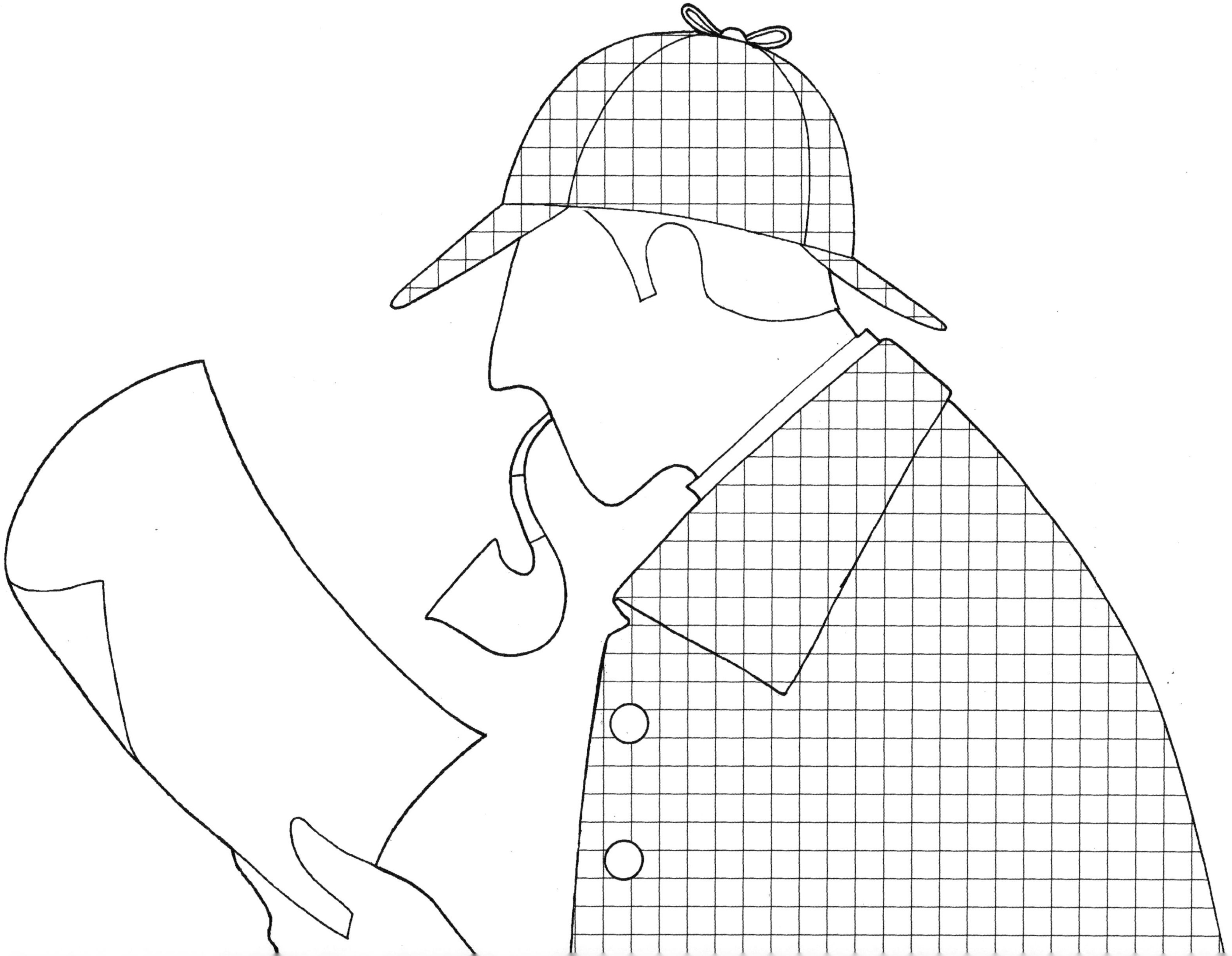

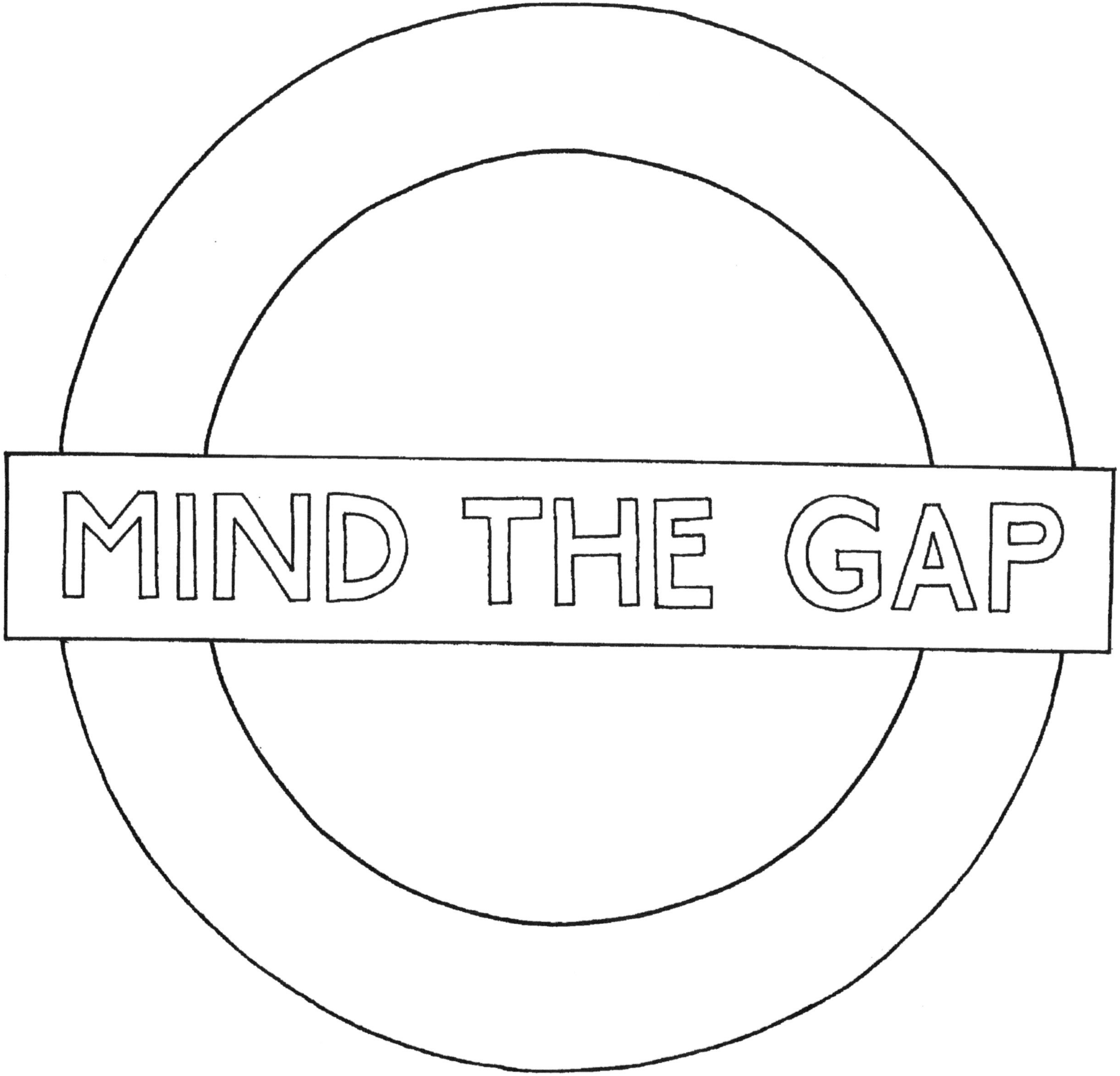
MIND THE GAP

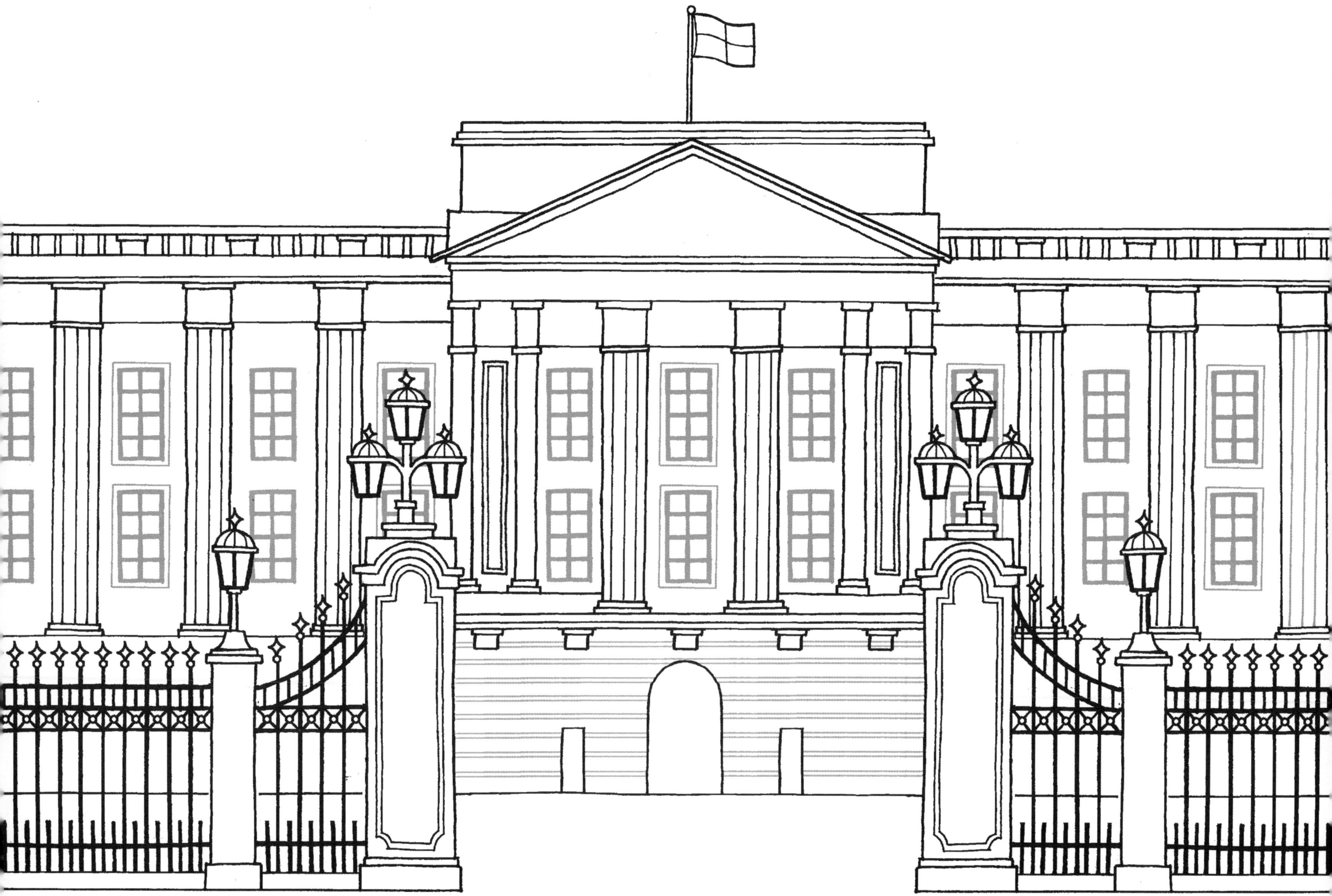

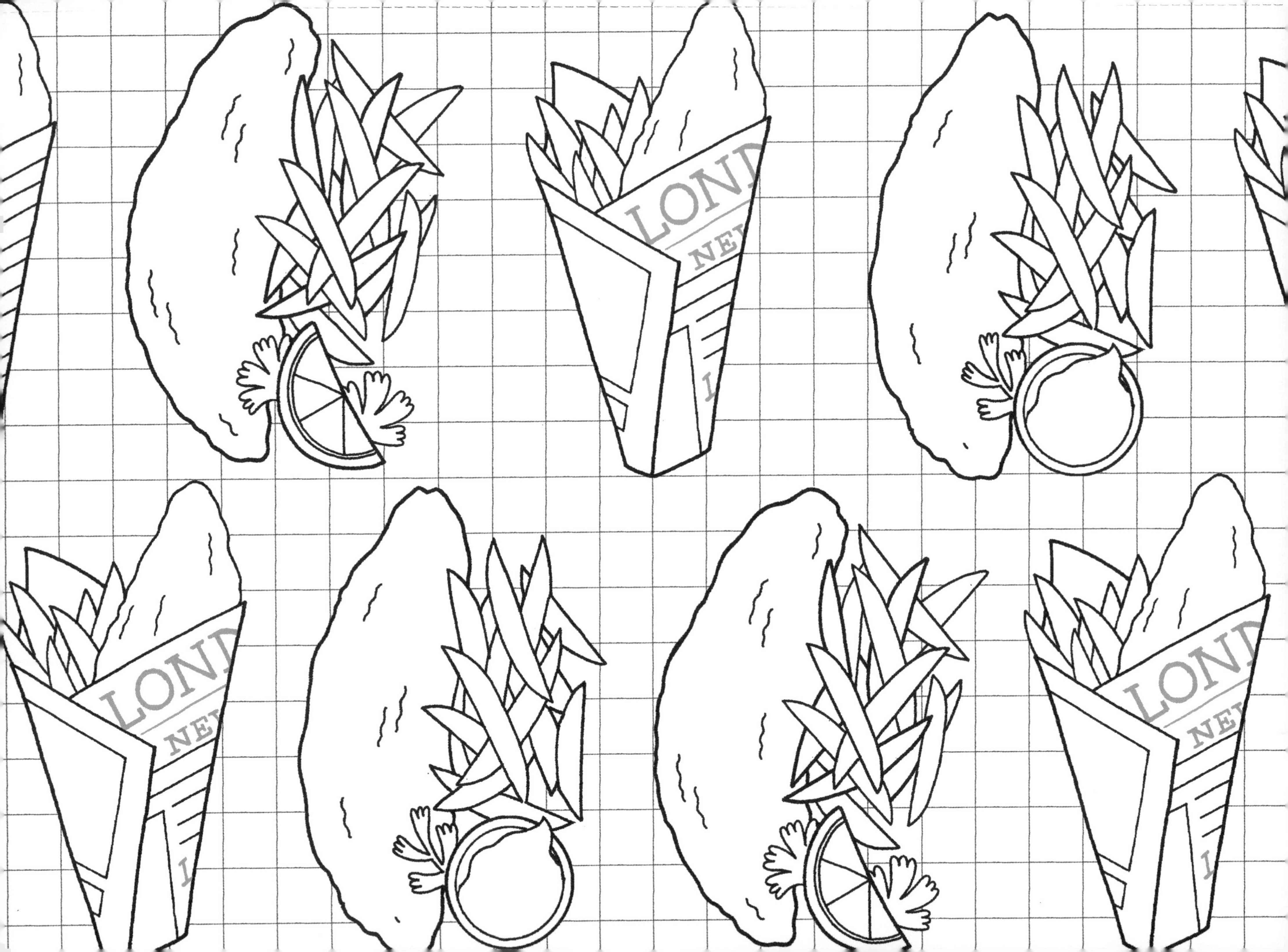

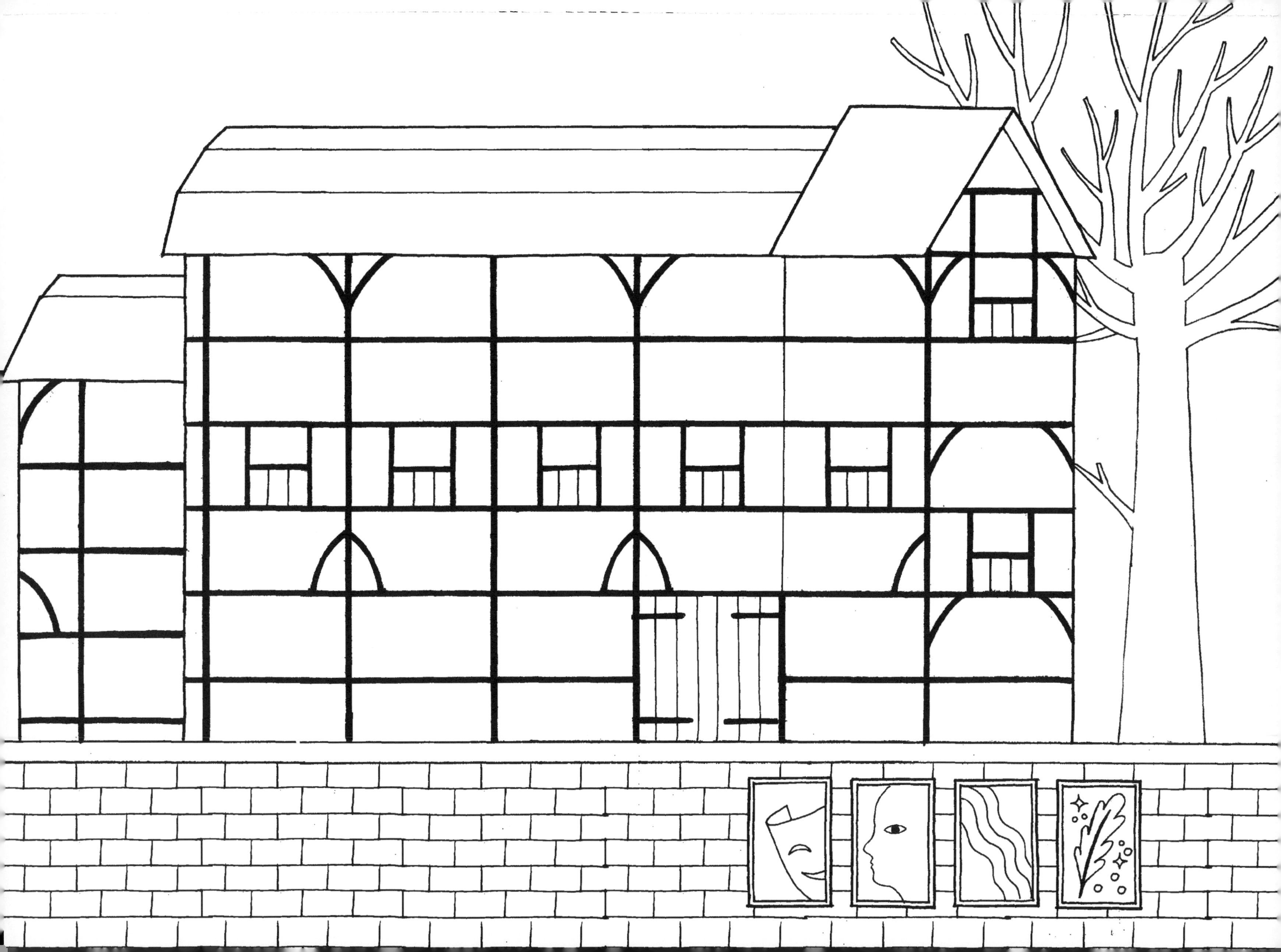

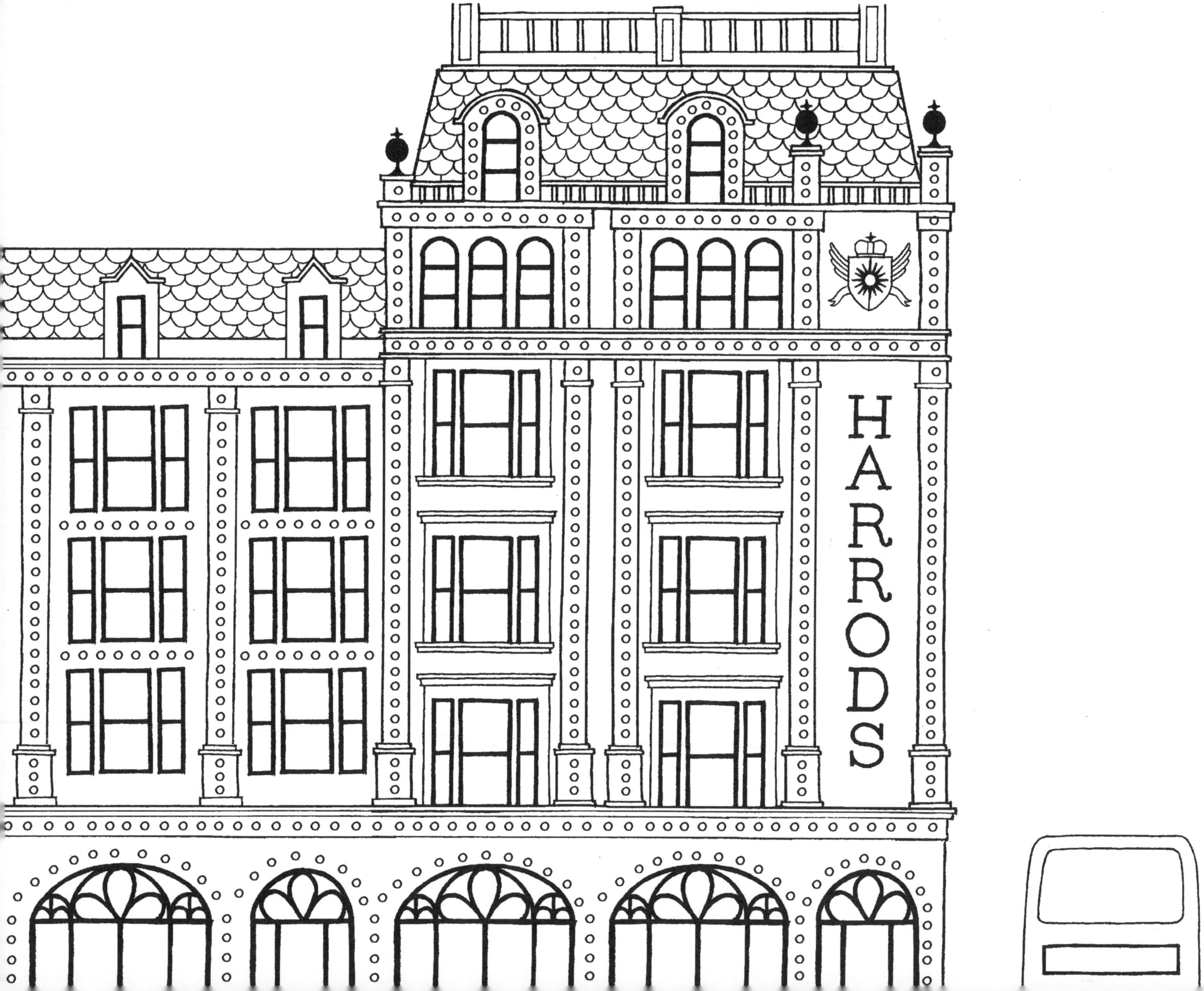
HARRODS

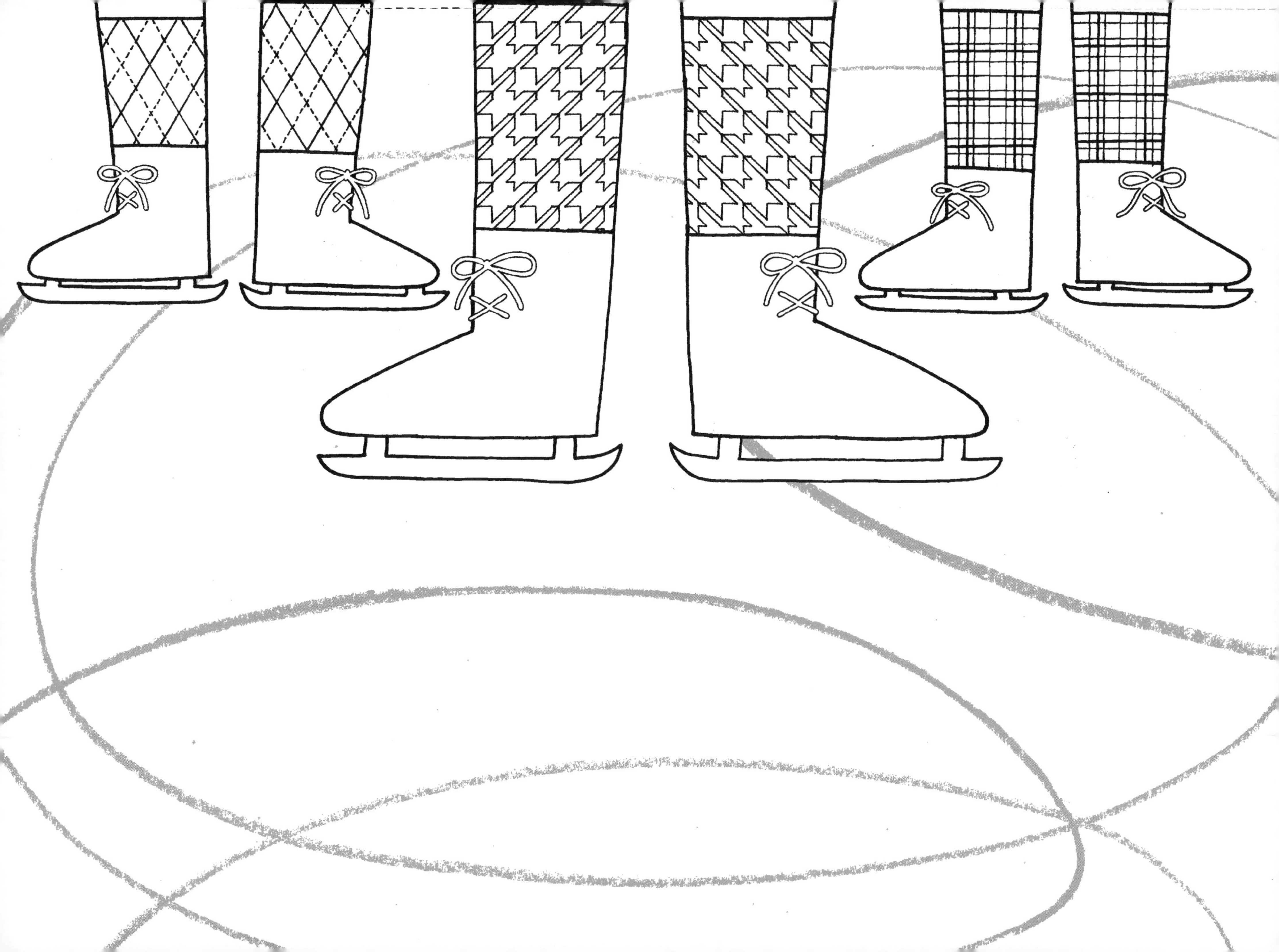

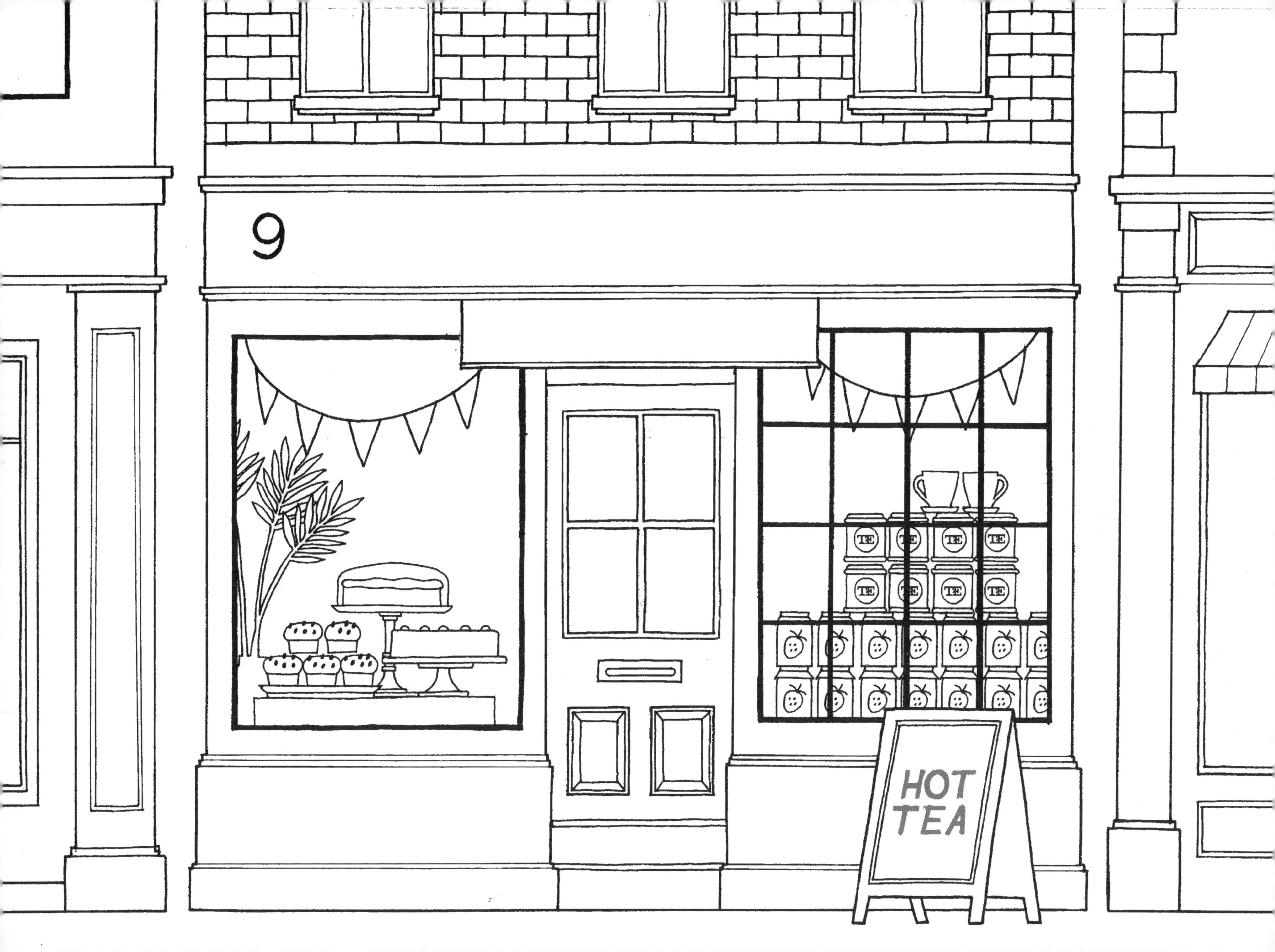
9
HOT
TEA

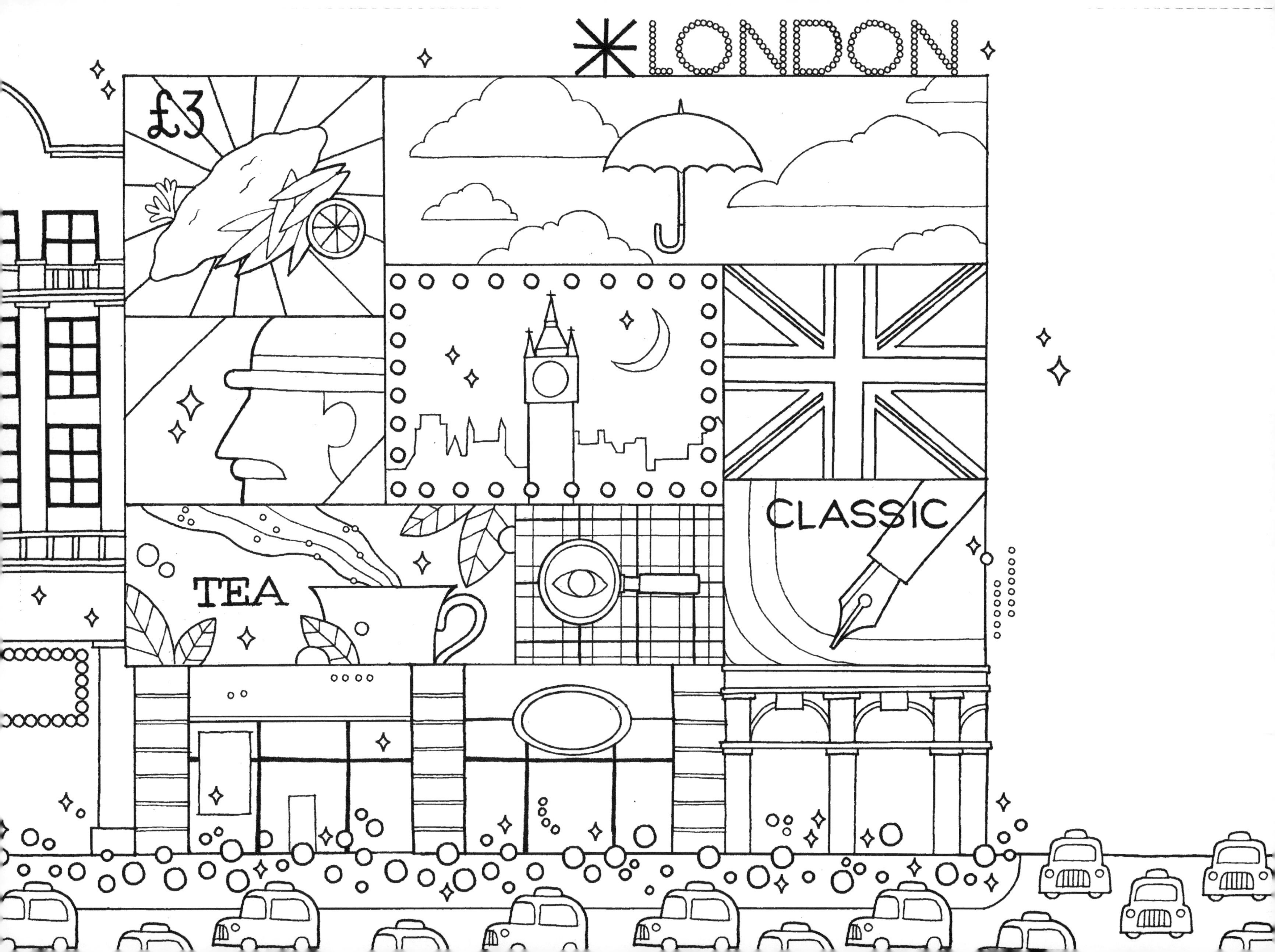
LONDON
£3
TEA
CLASSIC

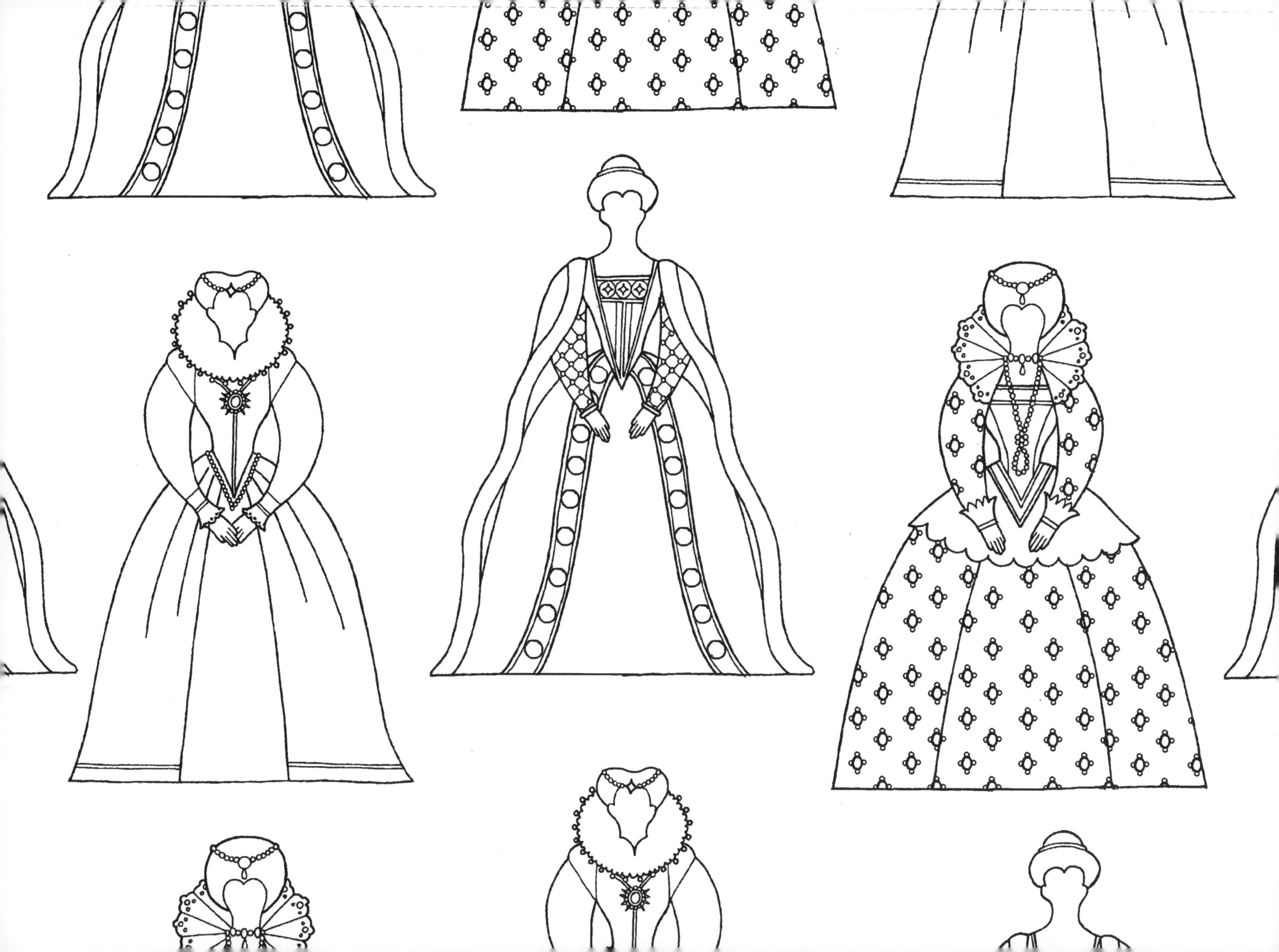

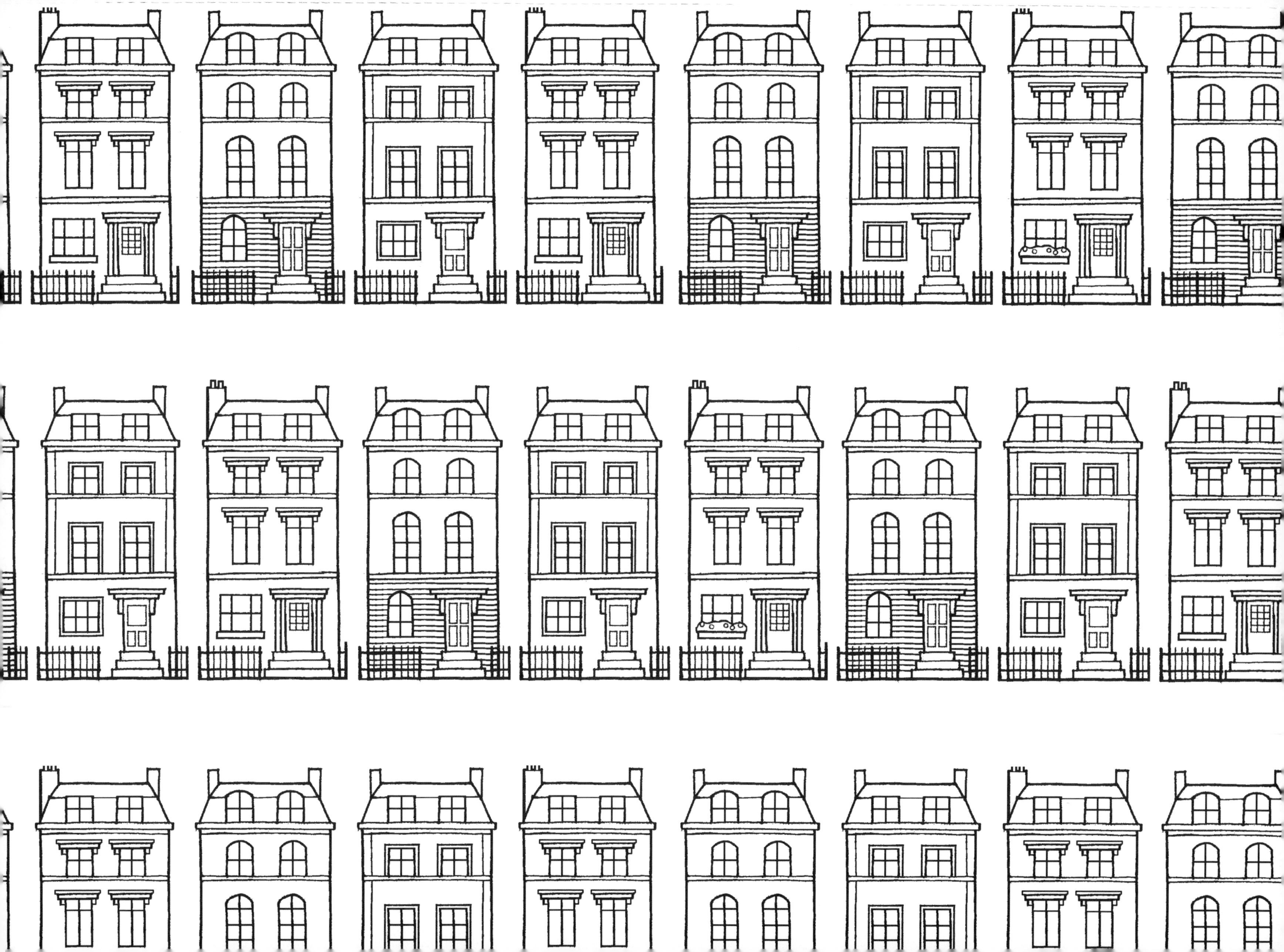

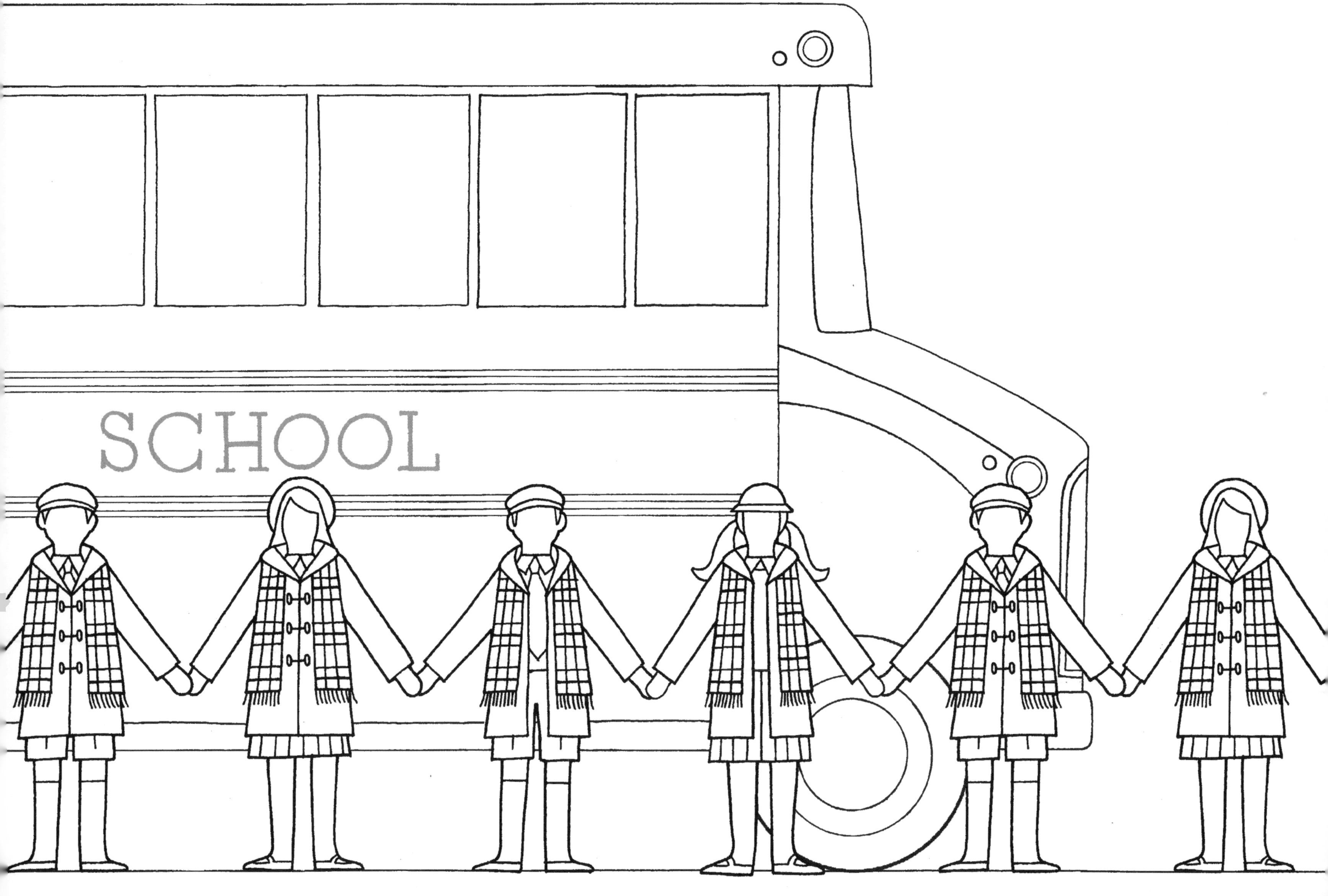
SCHOOL

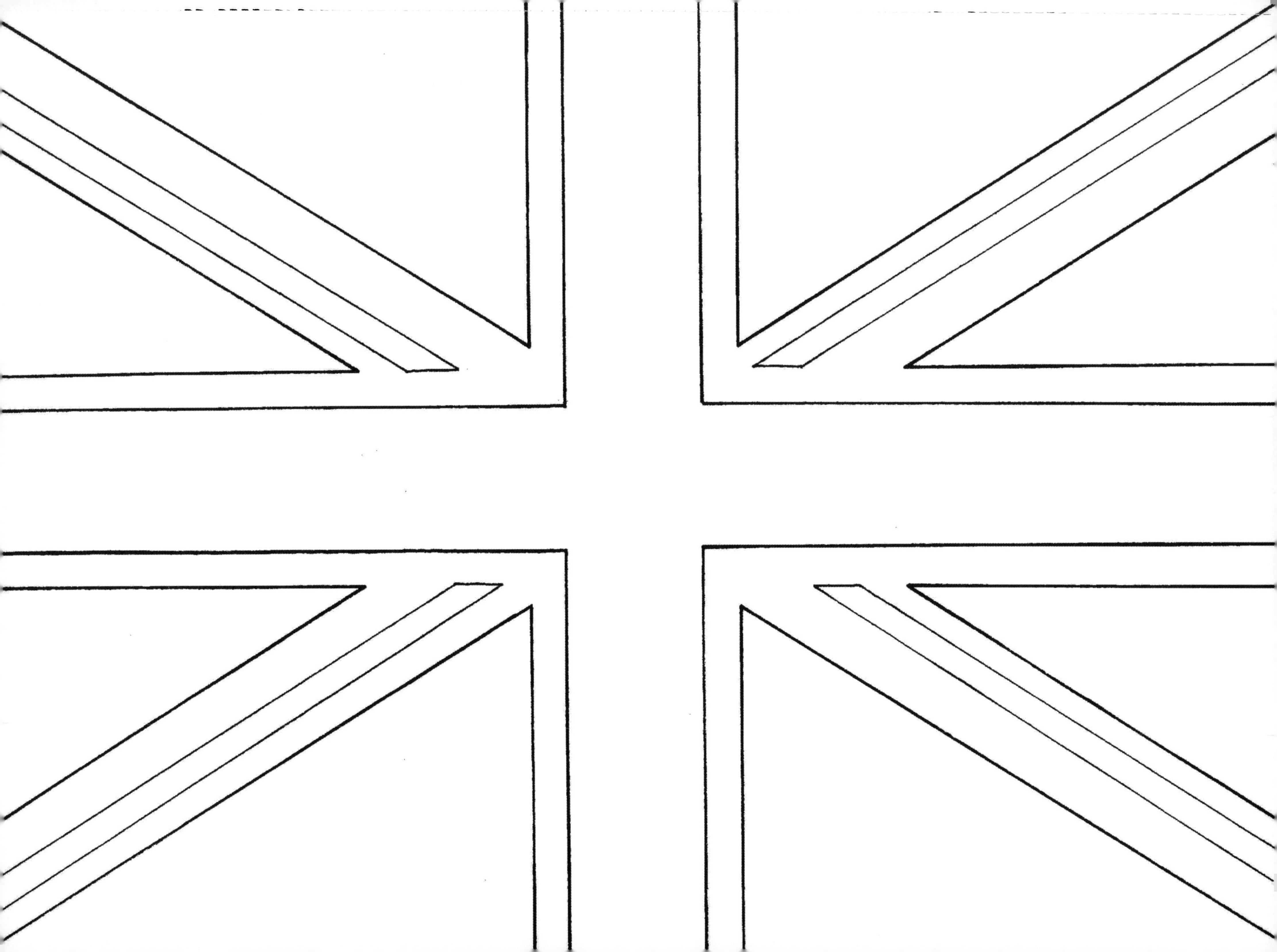

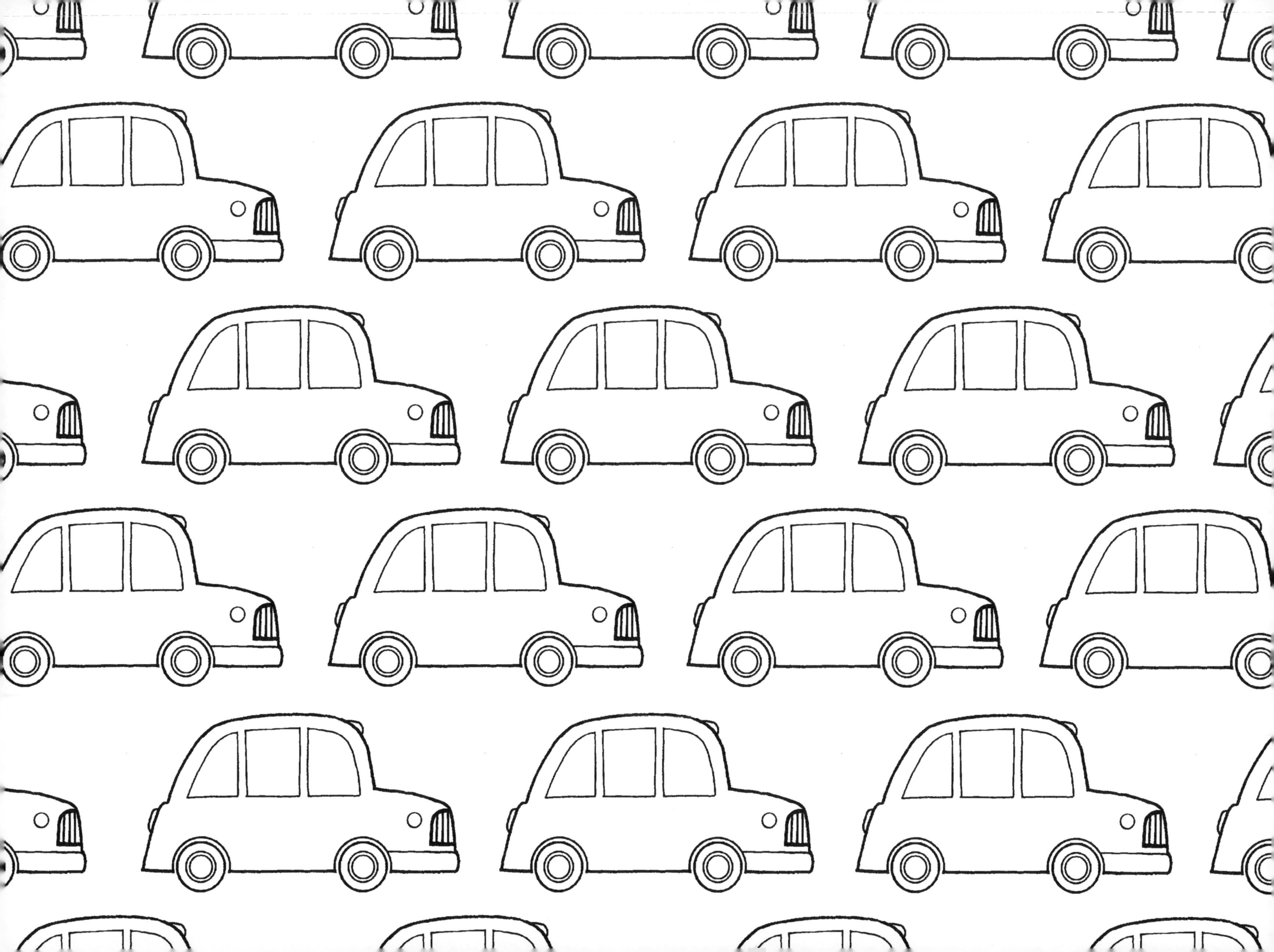

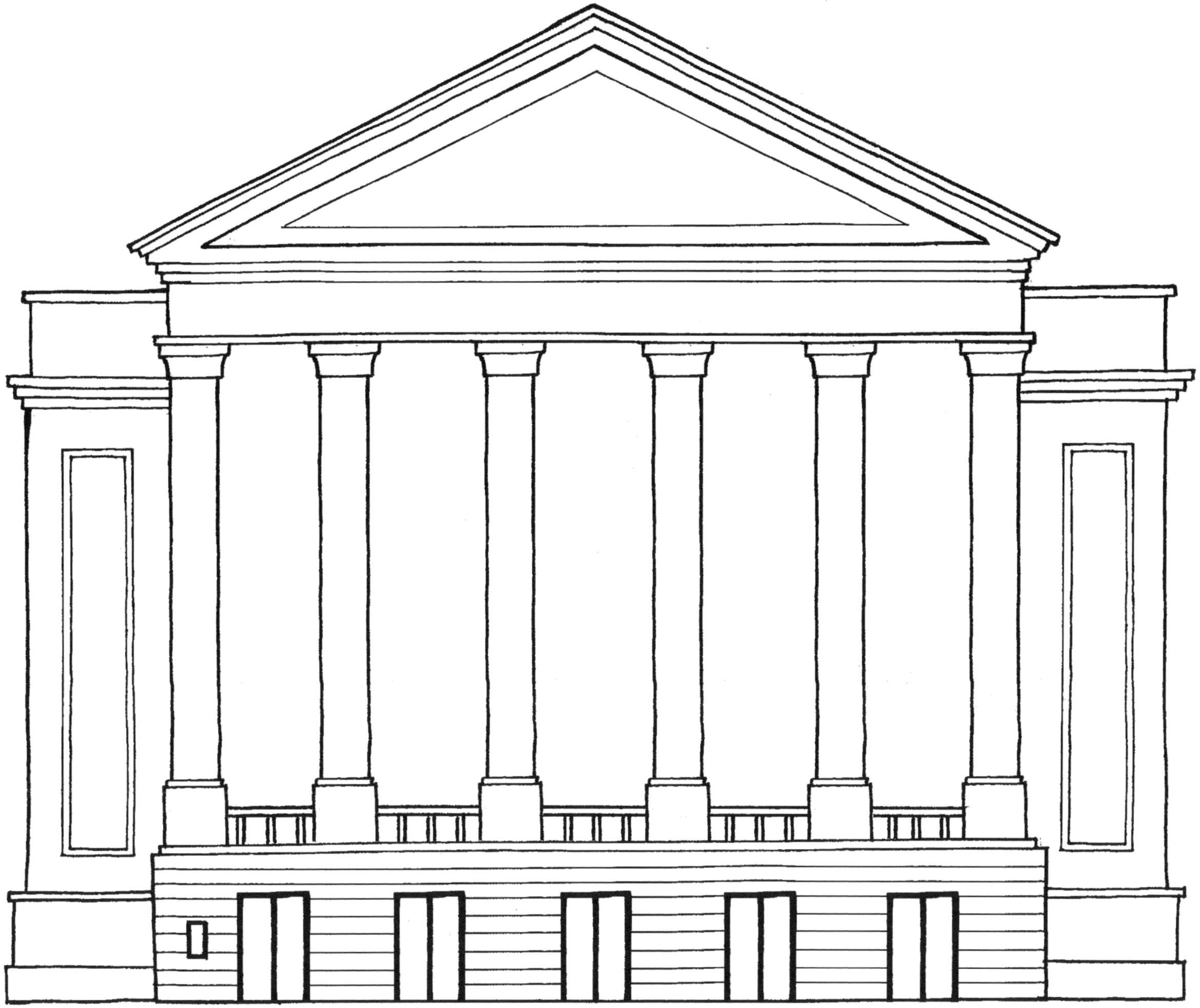

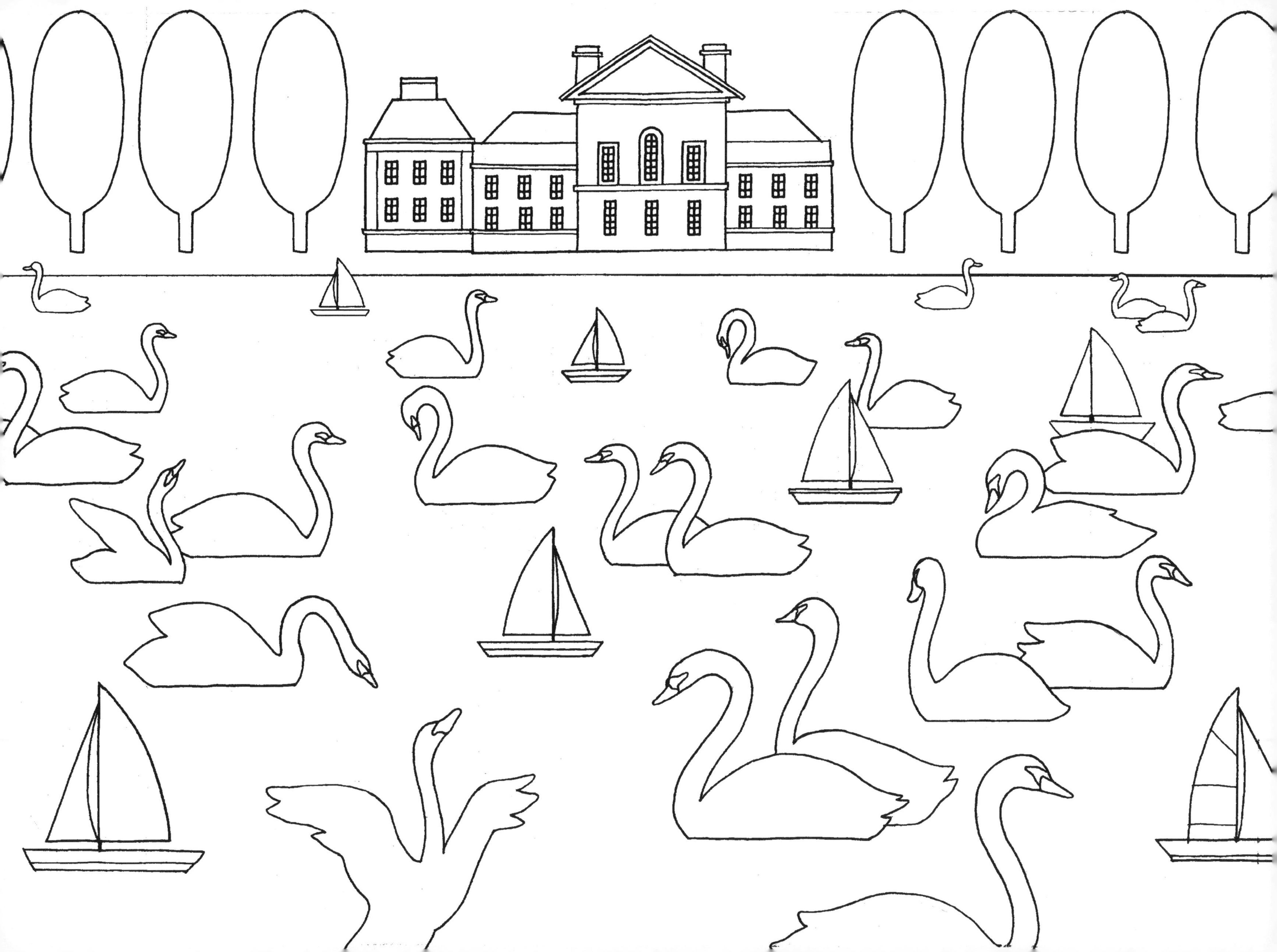

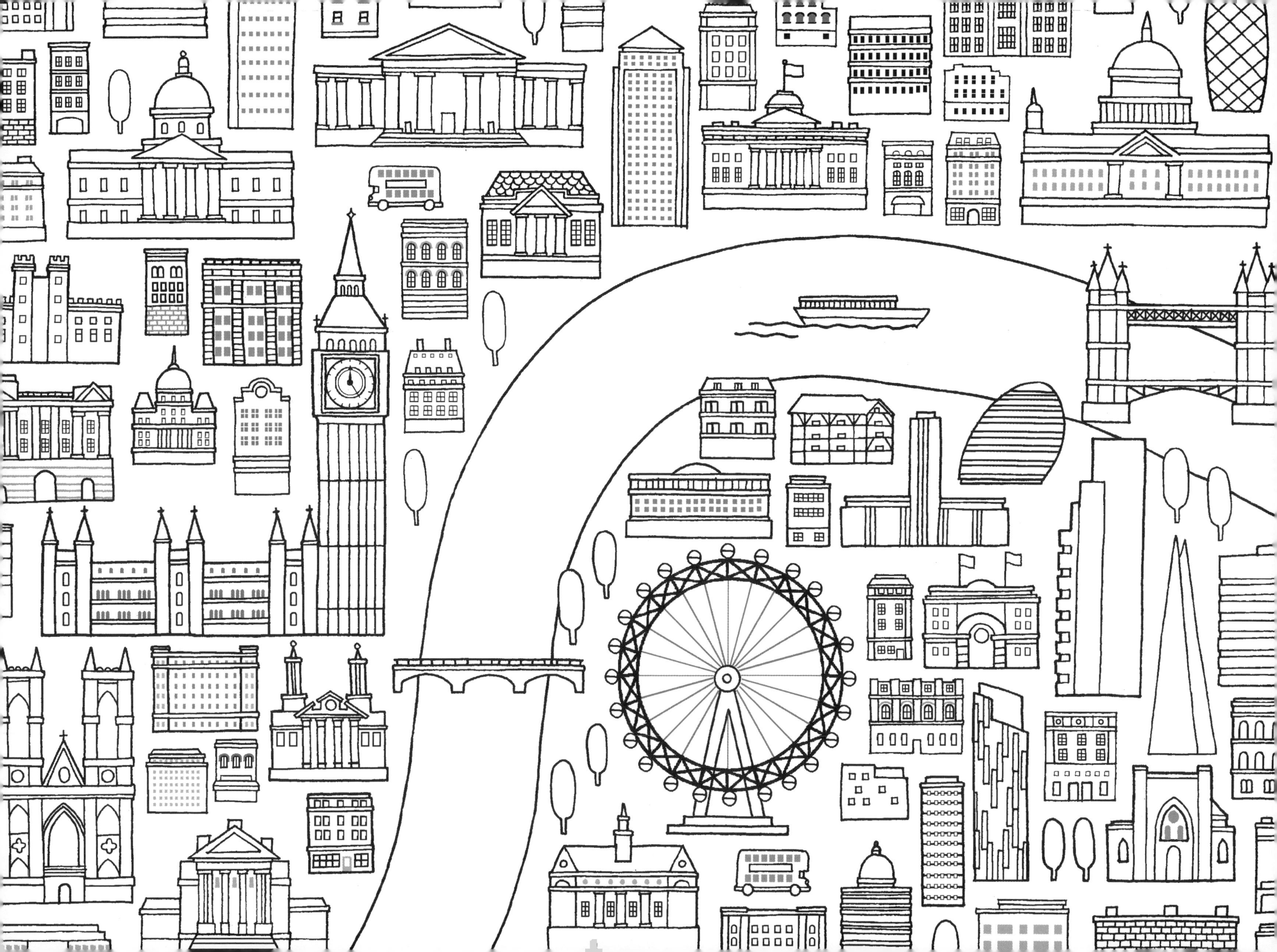